Marie Le Conte is a Frenc[...]
based in London. Raised [...]
in 2009 to study journalis[...]
publications, including the *Evening Standard and Dail[...]
News*. Since going freelance in 2017, she has written for
everyone from *GQ* and the *Guardian* to *VICE* and the *New
Statesman*, and frequently appears on radio and television.
Her first book, *Haven't You Heard? Gossip, Politics and Power* is
out now.

Praise for *Honourable Misfits*

'At a time when British politics is so depressing, it's a joy to
read about the follies of MPs in the past written with such
gusto and elan. Every politician should have a copy of this
by their bed and by the side of any other bed they may use'
Tony Robinson

'What a brilliant collection of characters – the wacky, the weird
and (occasionally) the wise. Marie makes history more fun than
it's meant to be. Dip in, and you won't be able to dip out'
Evan Davis

'This is something you didn't know you needed: a book to
make you strangely fond of MPs. At least, some MPs – and
all of them dead. At heart it is a very entertaining, affectionate celebration of weirdness, and a memorial to many
people who have almost completely been forgotten (some
of them rightly). And it will almost certainly make you feel
better about how YOUR career's going'
Mark Watson

Also by Marie Le Conte

Haven't You Heard?

Honourable Misfits

*A Brief History of Britain's Weirdest,
Unluckiest and Most Outrageous MPs*

MARIE LE CONTE

JOHN MURRAY

First published in Great Britain in 2021 by John Murray (Publishers)
An Hachette UK company

This paperback edition published in 2022

I

A CIP catalogue record for this title is available from the British Library

Paperback ISBN 978-1-529-34964-1
eBook ISBN 978-1-529-34965-8

Typeset in Bembo MT by Palimpsest Book Production Limited, Falkirk, Stirlingshire

Printed and bound in Great Britain by Clays Ltd, Elcograf S.p.A.

John Murray policy is to use papers that are natural,
renewable and recyclable products and made from wood grown in sustainable
forests. The logging and manufacturing processes are expected to conform
to the environmental regulations of the country of origin.

John Murray (Publishers)
Carmelite House
50 Victoria Embankment
London EC4Y 0DZ

www.johnmurraypress.co.uk

Contents

Introduction   1

1. The Eccentrics   7
2. The Unfortunate   57
3. The Adventurous   83
4. The Lustful and the Idle   121
5. The Outlaws and the Villains   145
6. The Assorted Mavericks   187

Acknowledgements   209
Bibliography   211

Introduction

This is not a book about politics. The pages that follow contain no insights on how one should be running the country, or on the laws that should be made, mended or repealed. It is not about Westminster, not really; the SW1 postcode merely provides a convenient backdrop.

This book is not about the people who have shaped this country and made it the place it is today. It is not about the heroes who protected Britain from those who wished it harm, or the ones who made life better for the millions at home. In fact, it is not about the vast majority of politicians, who perhaps never led but always tried to help when they could.

Instead, *Honourable Misfits* is about the men (and occasional women) who marched to the beat of their own drum. Some got quite a lot done in their lifetime; others not much at all. Most ended up being footnotes in history because of what they managed to achieve, often by accident, or simply because of their peculiar ways.

It is not a celebration of them, but it isn't a condemnation either. Instead, this walk through history's most eccentric politicians intends to make a point, namely that politics is weird, and that is because we are weird. We are ruled and represented by people we elect, and those people are us; if crooks, cranks and oddballs end up in Parliament, it is because enough of us are crooks, cranks and oddballs, and we are ruled by our own. There is a famous anecdote about Labour MP Bill Stones, who was once drinking a pint of ale in Parliament's Strangers' Bar when he heard someone complain that the Commons was full of cunts. 'There's plenty of cunts int' country,' he said, 'and they deserve some representation.'

Finally, this book aims to be a reminder of something that will sound glib written down but is nonetheless often forgotten; politicians are people. They are humans who often (but not always) try their best, who fail when they didn't mean to, and who sometimes do what is easy instead of what is good. They have peculiar obsessions, a tendency to self-sabotage, irrational likes and dislikes, and more flaws than you could count. So do I, and so do you. The people we are about to discuss represent not just the highs and the lows of humanity but mostly the weird corners, the shades of grey and the traits we'd rather forget we have.

Of course, they will mostly represent the excesses of those traits; it wouldn't be an entertaining topic to write or read about otherwise. But this does not mean they existed in a vacuum; there's plenty of misfits in this country, and are you sure you're not one of them?

～

This is probably the point where I should clarify what I mean by 'misfits'. What does the term generally mean? Well, it depends. As you will see, I have divided the MPs I have chosen to profile into six categories. Broadly speaking, there are some unfortunate ones, some adventurous ones, some lustful ones, and then and there are some villains, eccentrics, and everyone else. In parliamentary history as in life, it is impossible to neatly put people in boxes, and several MPs could have gone in several different categories; in the end I had to drop them into the one they were closest to.

This does not mean there is no overlap; some MPs did a lot of travelling but also a lot of fooling around during those travels, while others committed the occasional crime while mostly being a bit odd. You get the gist. On the topic of villains − it was not easy coming up with some straightforward rules on who to include and who to leave aside when it came to lawbreakers. Some crimes are so beyond the pale that they instantly disqualified the person who committed them, which is why you will not find any paedophiles in the chapters ahead. Similarly, I tried to keep the slave traders to a minimum, although one or two did make the cut as there were simply so many of them, once upon a time.

On a different but related note, many MPs were killed in cruel and brutal ways a few centuries ago, but few made the cut. For many centuries wars raged abroad and at home, and it was quite frequent for MPs to partake in them, with predictable consequences. In fact, the bar was set high when it came to death in office as, to put it bluntly, it was quite easy to die young for quite a long time in Britain. One shooting accident is a tragedy worthy of inclusion; dozens become a fact of life.

Speaking of Britain − as you may or may not know, depending on how interested you are in political history, the whole island of Ireland was represented in Westminster's Parliament for some time, and Ireland sent its fair share of extravagant MPs to the Commons. 'Britain' is a shorthand in the title, but I acknowledge that for some time the Houses of Parliament covered ground beyond today's borders.

It also seems worth mentioning that until relatively recently – in the grand scheme of things – parliamentary democracy was not what it is today. If you were a man of a certain background, it practically was a given that you could become a member of Parliament if you wanted to. Thanks to rotten (or 'pocket') boroughs, the 'electorate' was a handful of well-bred men – or a singular count or baron of some description – who could be easily won round. This is why several entries will mention someone yearning for a seat, then getting a seat without a campaign getting mentioned in between, as there was no campaign.

On the subject of the olden days; in case you have not guessed, what follows is not very diverse. In fact, I can even go further and say that what follows is tremendously male and tremendously pale, as these were the main characteristics of British lawmakers for a very, very long time. This could have been rectified by making the cast of characters more current, but this would be a different book. A peculiar death that took place three hundred years ago can only be funny in the way that that same death happening in the past twenty years wouldn't. Distance turns tragedy into farce, and the latter was what I sought.

Finally, it should be noted that this book does not cover all possible ground, in two different ways. Firstly, I do not pretend I managed to track down every single maverick who ever stepped foot in Parliament; many were lost to history, others became such myths it was impossible to disentangle fact from fiction, and a few probably just slipped through my net. If you can think of any, do let us know and we will see what we can do in the next edition. Secondly, the short biographies that follow are intended as just that: snapshots of people's lives, with a focus on what made them interesting.

In some cases, their quirks came out in Parliament, and little time will be spent on the lives they led outside of it; in others, what they did on the green benches was only a footnote in an otherwise fascinating existence, and so the Commons will barely be mentioned. If you wish to find out more about one of our MPs, there is plenty out there for you to read, and the bibliography at the end of this book is intended to provide you with a decent starting point.

In the meantime, I should probably get started, shouldn't I? Roll up, roll up! Do I have some misfits to introduce you to . . .

I

The Eccentrics

At one time, an honour to his nature; at another,
a satire on humanity.

Charles James Apperley ('Nimrod')
on the life of John 'Mad Jack' Mytton

John Bentinck (1800–79)

MP for King's Lynn, 1824–6

Some men are born eccentrics; odd children turning into peculiar teens and even weirder adults. Others take an unexpected turn at some point, and slide into eccentricity as they grow older. John Bentinck was the latter. Born in London, he was always known by his second name, John, as he shared his first name, William, with all the male members of his family.*

He was home-schooled and then joined the army at eighteen, serving in the 10th and 7th Royal Hussars, among other regiments, and eventually rising to the rank of captain. In 1822 his uncle George Canning offered to make him one of two personal private secretaries at the Foreign Office, alongside one of his brothers, but he turned down the offer. Sadly for Bentinck, politics was not done with him yet; in 1824 his elder brother – you guessed it – William died, making John the new Marquess of Titchfield. That same

---

* Why they didn't simply choose to switch all the first and second names around is a valid question, but sadly not one relevant to the topic at hand.

year it was agreed that he should run for King's Lynn in Parliament, as the seat was traditionally held by a member of the family.

He managed to last in the Commons for an impressive two years, given how little he did there, before standing down on grounds of ill-health and conveniently handing the seat on to his uncle. Though he had also had to leave the army because of his frail constitution, it seems fair to assume that Bentinck wasn't heartbroken to be leaving Westminster to go travelling instead. Somehow this was not the last he would see of the blasted building; in 1854 he became the fifth Duke of Portland after his father died. The title came with a seat in the House of Lords, which he was clearly so desperate to have that he only took the oath of allegiance a full three years later. And, for the sake of being thorough, it should be pointed out that he was offered the Order of the Garter not once but twice, and refused both times.

In any case, it was not in the areas of military service (he had a fairly decent military career) or politics (in which his career was largely non-existent) that Bentinck decided to shine. Instead, his crowning achievement was Welbeck Abbey, the north Nottinghamshire estate he inherited and trans-formed beyond recognition. Among others things, he presided over the building of:

- kitchen gardens covering nearly 9 hectares (or 22 acres) that were encased by high walls with recesses in which braziers were put to make the fruit ripen quicker
- a 1,000-feet-long peach wall

- a riding house that was 396 feet long, 108 feet wide and 50 feet high, which was lit using 4,000 gas jets.

And that's only what was above ground. Bentinck got his workers – mostly Irish labourers who had been building the London underground – to dig over a dozen miles of tunnels underneath Welbeck Abbey. The main tunnel was around a third of a mile long and was wide enough for two carriages to ride through side by side. It had gas lamps installed overhead, and led to a one and a quarter-mile pathway connecting the lodge and the south lodge. Then there was the Plant Corridor, which was just over half a mile long and wide enough that several people could walk through it together, and which connected the main house to the riding house. Running parallel to it was a narrower tunnel to be used by the servants.

Other tunnels included some smaller corridors with narrow-gauge rails used for transporting hot food (mostly chicken) throughout the estate, as well as the Horse Corridor, which was decorated with antler racks and led to the great hall. You see, Bentinck didn't only want to be able to travel underground; he wanted to be able to live underground too. The grandest of the rooms below ground was originally meant to be a chapel but ended up taking turns as a picture gallery and ballroom. It was 164 feet long and 65 feet wide, making it the largest private room in England when it was built, and had a ceiling painted like a sunset, bull's eye skylights and a hydraulic lift. If he ever got bored of it, he could always go to the subterranean library instead, the glass roof observatory or the underground billiards room.

As you may have guessed, building all this required a lot

of manpower; so much, in fact, that Bentinck ended up employing thousands of men over two decades. Perhaps surprisingly, given that he was a man of a certain time from a certain class, most writing from the era makes him sound like a fundamentally decent employer. He provided doctor's visits, food and fuel to employees who fell ill and to their families, and offered housing to widows, none of which were a given in the nineteenth century. He also provided each employee with 'an umbrella, a suit of clothes, a top hat, and a donkey' to facilitate comings and goings around the estate, and built his workers a roller-skating rink near the lake when the activity became fashionable.

There was, however, one hitch; Bentinck's staff were not allowed to interact with him, or even acknowledge him if he happened to walk past them. No, really; one of his employees once tipped his hat as he bumped into the owner of the estate and was promptly fired. In fairness, he was like that with everyone, and had grown to become a deeply introverted man, as opposed to a rude one. The only person allowed to interact with him face to face was his valet; everyone else had to make do with exchanges of letters. If he left his quarters, it was usually via a network of smaller tunnels he could walk through, so no one knew where he was or if he had decided to go for a wander.

Sometimes he would go for walks outside but only at night, with a female servant walking 40 yards ahead of him with a lantern. If he really did have to venture outdoors during the day, he would do so wearing a very tall hat, not one but two overcoats, and a very high collar, and would carry a huge umbrella. Rumours at the time swirled around the reasons for his behaviours, and he was thought to perhaps have a crippling skin condition, but there never was any evidence of it; as far as we can tell, Bentinck simply was, by the time he reached middle age, a very odd fellow.

In fact, the older he got, the more peculiar he became. By 1879, Welbeck Abbey had fallen into disrepair, apart from a suite of five rooms he still lived in, all of which had pink walls and barely any furniture. He moved back to London that year, where he died a few months later; he was buried in a simple grave in the Kensal Green cemetery.

John Benjamin Stone (1838–1914)

MP for Birmingham East, 1895–1910

John Benjamin Stone was born in Birmingham and spent the early years of his career in paper manufacturing and at his father's glass works. More importantly, he spent his form-ative years collecting photographs, prints, stereographs and anything else he could get his hands on. He was also a keen traveller in the 1860s, going as far as Norway and Lapland and buying all the pictures he could find there, though not taking any himself quite yet.

Back in England, he immersed himself in local politics, serving in town councils in Birmingham and then Sutton Coldfield, founding the Birmingham East Conservative Association and eventually being elected mayor of Birmingham. Unsurprisingly, he then made his way to the House of Commons in 1895 as the Conservative MP for Birmingham East.

Still, politics was only ever an aside in Stone's life. In

around 1888 he had started taking his own photographs, as the medium had become more accessible to people who weren't professional photographers. Well, relatively more accessible, as he originally had to employ two men full-time to work on his pictures. In any case, a passion was born, and Stone began to capture everything he could on camera.

Sometimes it would be scenes from foreign expeditions, including South Africa, the Middle East, Brazil – where he went to document a solar eclipse – and China. Sometimes, as he put it himself, he would set out to 'portray for the benefit of future generations the manners, customs, the festivals and pageants' of the era with a view to stimulating 'local patriotism', to draw out 'links with the past' and to 'add to everybody's knowledge of the country we love'. In practice, this meant travelling around the British Isles taking pictures of traditional customs and outfits.

Then there was the Palace of Westminster. Though parliamentarians had been very reluctant to let photographers into their workplace, the fact that Stone was an MP himself clearly worked in his favour. In his entirely unofficial capacity as the Commons' photographer, he spent a decade photographing everyone from his fellow MPs to House staff and visitors, gaining quite a public profile in the process. That he was mostly known for his pictures and not his political work didn't seem to bother him too much; when a reporter once cheekily asked him if his position as an MP ever interfered with his photography career, he replied 'only to a small extent'.

By that point the press had affectionately given him a series of nicknames, from Sir Kodak, after the camera he used, to Sir Snapshot and the Knight of the Camera. Still, his amateur career reached its peak in 1911, when he was hired as the official photographer of the coronation of King George V. Most of his life was in Westminster by this point, but that did not mean he had left the rest of the world behind. After having spent several years as an early president of the Birmingham Photographic Society and having helped found the Warwickshire Photographic Survey, he launched the National Photographic Records Association in 1897.

It had collapsed by the time of the coronation, but had managed to print thousands of photographs – most taken by Stone himself – which had been deposited at the British Museum. When he died, in 1914, Sir Benjamin Stone left a collection of over twenty-five thousand pictures behind, a lot of which are still shown in museums today. This would certainly please him: as he once explained, 'I have aimed at recording history with the camera, which, I think, is the best way of recording it.'

Ronald Gower (1845–1916)

MP for Sutherland, 1867–74

If you have been to Stratford-upon-Avon, you may have encountered the Shakespeare memorial, a collection of bronze statues representing the playwright as well as several of his most famous characters. What you may not know is that the artist was an MP, and that there was a lot more to his life than these few statues.

The youngest son of eleven children, Ronald Gower went, as most sons of dukes did, to Eton, then Cambridge. At twenty-one he stood for Parliament in Sutherland as a Liberal candidate and won. Young Gower wasn't exactly fascinated by politics, though he was soon referred to as 'the beautiful boy' of the House. When Gladstone's government came to an end in 1874, he stood down – 'with some relief', according to some – and got to focus on his real passion: the arts.

He already had been a frequent visitor of artists' studios – including Garibaldi's in Italy – but formally got more involved that year when he was appointed as a trustee of the National Portrait Gallery. Still, this was not enough; Gower yearned to make some art himself, and had tried his hand at painting, etching and photography, but with little success. This changed when he went to Paris a year later and joined the studio of sculptor Albert-Ernest Carrier-Belleuse, one of the founding members of the Société Nationale des Beaux Arts.

Eventually moving to his own studio with Carrier's assistant Luca Madrassi, Gower started his career as a sculptor in earnest with, among other works, a full-length figure of Marie Antoinette on her way to the guillotine. Soon enough he moved on to his Shakespeare project, which took several years and which he funded himself. Though it took some convincing originally, Gower managed to place his statues in Stratford, with an inauguration taking place in October 1888. Deciding that the work was his magnum opus, he swore off sculpting afterwards and dedicated the rest of his life to writing and travelling.

To be fair to him, he did have a colourful personal life to keep him busy. A gay man, Gower was an acquaintance of Oscar Wilde and is widely thought to have been the inspiration for Lord Henry Wotton in *The Picture of Dorian Gray*. Despite the (ironically named) magazine *Man of the World* accusing him of having relations with men in 1879 – and the

Prince of Wales calling him 'a member of an association for unnatural practices' – Gower's secret remained fairly safe.

His name was also mentioned in the press during the Cleveland Street scandal of 1889, when a gay brothel was discovered by the police, but enough powerful men were linked to the place that his presence remained largely unnoticed. In fact, Gower met the man who would become his long-term partner four years later. Journalist Frank Hird was nicknamed the Bébé because of his relative youth; he was twenty when the pair met. The age gap worked in their favour in the end, as Gower adopted Hird in order to regularise their relationship, which allowed them to live together.

Sadly, financial ruin interrupted the couple's bliss in 1913, when Francis Shackleton – the brother of famous explorer Ernest – defrauded Gower of his fortune by getting him to purchase some dodgy shares. Gower had to sell his country house as a result, but at least he and Hird stayed together until he died.

Only in his forties by that point, Frank Hird ended up marrying a woman a few years later. When he died, his body was laid to rest next to Lord Gower; when she died, her ashes were buried with the two of them.

Richard Heber (1773–1833)

MP for Oxford University, 1821–6

Richard Heber loved books from a young age. During his school days he tried to buy so many of them that his father irritably wrote to him:

I cannot say I rejoice in the importation of the cargo of books you mention from abroad, we had before enough and too many, ten times more than were ever read or even looked into. Of multiplying books . . . there is neither end nor use. The cacoethes of collecting books draws men into ruinous extravagancies. It is an itch which grows by indulgence and should be nipped in the bud.

It was a valiant effort that failed entirely. While attending Brasenose College, Oxford, Heber edited the works of Roman orator and poet Silius Italicus and expanded his literary tastes and collection. In fact, his father's death in 1804 brought his bibliophilia to new heights. Having inherited large estates in Yorkshire and Shropshire, he now had enough space to indulge his frenetic search for rare and special books. It probably didn't help that one edition was rarely enough for him; as he himself put it, 'no gentleman can be without three copies of a book: one for show, one for use, and one for borrowers'.

Another interest Heber had was politics: though he only became the MP for Oxford University in 1821, he first stood for the seat in 1806, and unsuccessfully ran several times after that. It is especially peculiar, then, that once he finally got into the House of Commons, he did very little there. According to a piece published at the time, his performance was 'by no means answerable to the expectations of many of his constituents'. Though he did vote fairly frequently, he rarely made himself heard in the Chamber.

Heber was also one of the founders of the private members' club the Athenaeum in 1824. This didn't please his constituency, as the university had its very own club just around the corner. A year later, the provost of Oriel College pleaded with him to make the 'trifling sacrifice' of giving 'some public evidence of attention to the political feelings of the University', but, as his father had found decades before, there was little point trying to argue with Richard.

On the bright side, it must have been a relief for everyone when, later that year, Heber decided to stand down from the Commons. In fact, he had by that point left Britain altogether and taken up life on the Continent. In a particularly honest letter to his half-sister, he explained: 'Towards this I have been turning onward for some time and the impending dissolution seemed the proper moment to decide. Not taking an active part in its proceedings, I found the House somewhat of a fag and a bore and the time it took up unprofitably spent.'

Well, perhaps not entirely honest. Though it may well have been possible that he wanted to explore the distant, exotic lands of Antwerp, Heber had also been caught that summer making advances to two young men at the Athenaeum. This got back to the father of one of them, and then travelled all the way to the ears of then Home Secretary Robert Peel and his under-secretary Henry Hobhouse. Though Heber had initially denied the allegations, he did confess eventually, and was made to make a swift exit from London by Hobhouse.

His resignation raised some eyebrows, but the fact that he had been a less than stellar MP anyway provided a decent enough excuse for his decision. Or, as Peel put it to a concerned party in 1826, 'Heber was so listless last session, and appeared to have such a horror of anything which might by possibility call him up in the House of Commons, that I am hardly surprised at his resignation.'

Still, Sunday paper the *John Bull* decided to pour some petrol on the flames later that year by reporting that Heber was not to come back to England anytime soon, mentioning as well his 'over addiction to Hartshorn'. To the average reader, this must have seemed absurd; salt of hartshorn is a type of smelling salts made from deer antler. People in the know, however, would have noticed that Hartshorn was also the last name of a nineteen-year-old antiquary – Charles Henry Hartshorn – who had spent some months living with Heber. The message was clear; word of his homosexuality was still spreading, and he should stay away from London. Poor Hartshorn sued the mag for libel and won, but could not convince Heber to come back.

Maybe that was because he had found a way to occupy himself in exile; instead of chasing books in England, he now chased books across Europe, occasionally purchasing entire libraries in one go. On top of his houses in the mother-land, he had large depots in France, Belgium, the Netherlands and Germany. Still, the end of his life was a sad one; having returned to Pimlico in 1831, Heber spent his last two years a recluse and died alone.

As for his collection, it was found after his passing to total just under 150,000 books between several countries, including eight houses in England. They were all sold at a series of events in Paris, London and Ghent.

James Morrison (1789–1857)

MP for St Ives, 1830–1

MP for Ipswich, 1831–4

MP for Ipswich, 1835–7

MP for Inverness Burghs, 1840–7

James Morrison had humble beginnings. The son of a Hampshire innkeeper, his career took off when his parents died and he was sent to live with the Flints, some relatives who worked as haberdashers in London. According to a contemporary, he 'remodelled the whole system of the shop in a way so advantageous in its results that he naturally expected to become a partner'. Sadly the Flints wouldn't let it happen, so instead he went to work with the Todd family, who owned a similar shop. There, 'being a handsome as well as a clever man, he soon made himself necessary, and captivated Miss Todd, whom he married, and was taken in partnership'.

Everything was going great for James Morrison, and it was only the beginning. In 1817 he started travelling to Europe to establish some trade contracts, and by 1824 he had become the sole managing partner of the company and bought out his father-in-law, renaming the (very successful) business James Morrison & Company. Since being on the path to becoming richer than God was not enough for him, he also stood for Parliament a few times, eventually winning a seat in 1830.

According to parliamentary records, he wasn't the most impressive of MPs, and 'spoke infrequently and tended to overburden his speeches with financial detail'. That being said, he was 'respected from the outset as an expert on trade, manufacturing and finance', voted fairly often and sat on several select committees. Still, his real passion remained the realm of business.

According to fellow merchant John Bowring, Morrison 'established one of the largest and most lucrative concerns that has ever existed in London', earning the nickname the Napoleon of Shopkeepers. There are many theories on how he did that; the most famous is perhaps that his motto was 'small profits and quick returns', which allowed him to work with small margins but at increasingly large scales.

Then there are the quirkier stories about his particularly shrewd practices. He was said, for example, to have bought up all the black crêpe in the country as the health of Caroline of Brunswick, the queen consort, was deteriorating. When she finally passed weeks later, mourners only had one man to turn to. There was also the time he (allegedly) managed to avoid paying import taxes on leather gloves he was bringing in from France. When a huge shipment arrived in Southampton, the trader was asked to pay what he was due; Morrison refused, and told the customs officer to keep the cargo.

Said cargo was eventually put up for auction, but who could possibly want it? Instead of pairs, it was merely thousands of right-handed gloves. You see, Morrison had made two shipments, one to Southampton and another to Great Yarmouth, and so he was able to bid for both lots for practically no money. By the end of it, he had got hold of all his gloves without paying a penny in tax.

Though this perhaps wasn't the most honest way of doing business, it clearly worked for him. By the end of his life, Morrison owned land in Berkshire, Buckinghamshire,

Glamorgan, Hampshire, Essex, Middlesex, Oxfordshire, Kent, Surrey, Sussex, Wiltshire, Yorkshire and Scotland, as well as the island of Islay in the Inner Hebrides. His fortune was estimated at around £5 million when he passed away in 1857 – around half a billion pounds in today's money – making him the richest commoner of his time.

Joseph Brotherton (1783–1857)

MP for Salford, 1832–57

Oddly for a man who would spend so much of his life so dearly attached to Salford, Joseph Brotherton was actually born in Derbyshire. His family only moved to Lancashire in 1789 so his father could establish a cotton and silk mill in the area. A studious child, Brotherton taught himself French, science, philosophy and shorthand, and joined his father's business in 1802.

When his father died in 1809, Joseph took control of the mill. Ten years later, at the age of thirty-six, he decided he had made enough money to leave the business altogether – after all, cotton and silk had never been his true passion. In 1805 Brotherton had joined the Swedenborg Church, renamed the Bible Christian Church in 1809. The Nonconformist church encouraged its members to be vegetarians and tee-totallers, which he and his wife strictly adhered to. In fact, she published *Vegetable Cooking*, thought to be the first ever vegetarian cookbook, in 1812, while he wrote *On Abstinence from Intoxicating Liquors* in 1821, which was the first teetotal tract published in Britain.

Despite becoming the deacon of the church in 1816, Brotherton had by that point found yet another passion. A year earlier he joined the Little Circle, a group of Nonconformist liberals based in Manchester. Formed by cotton merchant John Potter, the group included among its members Potter's son Thomas, who would go on to become the first mayor of Manchester, parliamentary reformer Absalom Watkin and founder of the *Manchester Guardian* John Edward Taylor.

Among other things, the group fought for a parliamentary inquiry into the Peterloo Massacre and for better representation for industrial cities like Manchester and Leeds in the House of Commons. Their efforts weren't in vain; the Reform Act passed in 1832, and Brotherton was elected as Salford's first ever MP. Understandably grateful, the constituency returned him five times, including twice unopposed. To be fair to him, he also was a dedicated MP: during his time on the green benches he campaigned for more factory regulation, a ten-hour working day, better working-class education and the expansion of local government. In line with his religious beliefs, he was one of the first ever MPs to speak against the death penalty and he also set up a select committee on the effects of alcohol on society. That other MPs referred to the latter as 'the drunken committee' shows how seriously the endeavour was taken in Parliament. Still, its impressively forward-thinking report from 1834 called for

the establishment, by the joint aid of the government and the local authorities, and residents on the spot, of public walks and gardens, or open spaces for athletics and healthy exercises in the open air, in the immediate vicinity of every town, of an extent and character adapted to its population, and of district and parish libraries, museums and reading rooms, accessible at the lowest rate of charge.

It fell on deaf ears, unsurprisingly, but at least they tried. It is worth mentioning that Brotherton had some victories as well: in 1850 he was a supporter of the Public Libraries Bill, once again backing accessible education and calling libraries 'the cheapest police that could be established'. Closer to home, he had been instrumental in helping Salford set up a library, an art gallery and a museum, becoming the first local authority to do so.

Brotherton also set up the Vegetarian Society in 1847, as well as vegetarian soup kitchens to deal with the city's food shortages that same year, so it really isn't hard to see why he was so popular in the area. In a bittersweet turn of events, he died from a sudden heart attack in 1857 and was buried in the Weaste cemetery, which he had campaigned to open. The funeral procession was two and a half miles long, and his interment was the first to take place there.

Edward Watkin (1819–1901)

MP for Great Yarmouth, 1857

MP for Stockport, 1864–8

MP for Hythe, 1874–95

If you are the sort of person who is, for some reason, incredibly fond of trains, you may have heard of Edward Watkin already. Born in Salford, his career started in his father's mill business, then as a campaigner against the Corn Laws and co-founder of the *Manchester Examiner*.

In 1845 he became the secretary of the Trent Valley Railway, which marked the beginning of a lifelong obsession. In 1846 he became the assistant of the general manager of the London and North Western Railway, and in 1852 he went travelling around North America, then wrote a book about its railways. A year later he became general manager of the Manchester, Sheffield and Lincolnshire Railway, and . . . well, you get the gist.

In 1857 he entered Parliament as a Liberal MP, but despite his support for Manchester Liberalism he didn't feel the need to always support the same party. Not content with Gladstone's leadership, Watkin even flirted with taking the Conservative whip in 1880, and was at one point considered a Tory, a Liberal and an independent all at once. This was partly because he was a genuinely independently minded MP – he was against Irish Home Rule but in favour of giving women the vote, for example – but partly because there was only one thing he really cared about.

By 1881, Watkin had become the director of nine railway companies (including one in New York) and a trustee of a tenth. By that point his ambitions had also gone beyond mere railway tracks: in 1880 he had started work on a train tunnel under the Channel. Amusingly (though perhaps unsurprisingly), his plan wasn't even to connect London to France; what he was aiming for was to directly connect Manchester to Paris.

The idea was a good one, and he was already on the board of Chemin de Fer du Nord, the French railway company his English trains would have been connected to. While his company started digging at Shakespeare Cliff near Folkestone, he went on a PR offensive to convince England's elites that the idea was a good one. This probably explained why he took care never to attach himself too closely to one political party – as fellow MP Aretas Akers-Douglas once observed, 'no one knew what his politics were, except that he had voted for anyone or anything to get support for his Channel Tunnel'.

Despite managing to host the Archbishop of Canterbury, William Gladstone and the Prince and Princess of Wales at an underground champagne reception in the tunnel, his efforts were in vain. Many prominent figures feared that the tunnel could be used by the French to invade England, and the whole project was eventually blocked by Parliament, then cancelled altogether because of national security concerns.

While this was an obvious disappointment to Watkin, he had more (train-related) tricks up his sleeve. One of his companies had been working on extending the Metropolitan Railway towards the north-western suburbs of London. Still, getting trains to new places was one thing; convincing people to get on those trains was quite another. This is why he launched a large amusement park in Wembley in 1894, to go with the shiny new Wembley Park station that had opened a year previously.

Of course, it wasn't enough for the new park to have a boating lake or pleasure gardens; Watkin wanted it to include the tallest man-made structure in the world. That the Eiffel Tower had recently opened in Paris and was at that point the tallest building in the world was no coincidence. In fact, Watkin had tried to get Gustave Eiffel to build his tower, but he had politely declined fearing (not unreasonably) that his French compatriots wouldn't take kindly to him building an even bigger tower in another country. It did not stop Watkin.

Instead, he launched a design competition with a handsome prize of 500 guineas for the winner, which was won by London architects Stewart, McLaren & Dunn. The first layer of the tower – four legs supporting a 155 feet high platform – was built by 1896, but it revealed a very inconvenient problem. The ground in Wembley was marshy and muddy, and the nascent tower was ominously leaning. Given that the finished building was supposed to be 1,148 feet tall, this was not an encouraging sign.

There was also the small issue of Londoners having little interest in going to Wembley, and, if they did, not wanting to pay to go up the original platform. With construction not looking like it would start again anytime soon, the tower started gaining unflattering nicknames, including Shareholders' Dismay, London Stump and, perhaps more famously, Watkin's Folly. The whole project remained in limbo for several years, and its future was still uncertain when Watkin died in 1901. A year later it was deemed unsafe for the public, and in 1904 it was destroyed.

Though Watkin would have been sad to find out that the last big project of his life never did go anywhere, he perhaps would have found some solace in the fact that the Empire Stadium (later renamed Wembley Stadium) was built on those grounds and now attracts hundreds of thousands of day trippers to the area every year. It wasn't what he had in mind, but people did start flocking to the neighbourhood after all.

John Mytton (1796–1834)

MP for Shrewsbury, 1819–20

The (short, eventful) life of John Mytton is a great example of why you can really have too much of a good thing. In his case, the good thing was money; more precisely, the vast estate, many assets and annual income his father left him when John was only two years old. Perhaps his personality was always going to be an issue, but how would you behave if, as a toddler, you'd inherited a family seat worth over £4 million in today's money and an annual income equivalent to nearly £800,000?

We will never know how Mytton would have behaved had he had more humble beginnings. What we do know is that he went to Westminster School but was expelled after a year because of a fight with one of his tutors in the school grounds. He moved on to Harrow School, but they also kicked him out after three terms. A series of private tutors were then hired to try and give some education to the child, with relatively little success as he mostly enjoyed pranking them. Though we do not have records of everything he did, that he once left a horse in his tutor's bedroom* should give you an idea of what it was like to try and teach him.

Of course he was very rich, so none of this really mattered. In 1816 he started studying for a degree at Trinity College, Cambridge, although the fact that he brought 339 gallons of port with him to the university tells you how much

---

* Fair play to him though, that's a great prank.

studying he intended to do. That he left without a degree to go travelling instead should not come as a surprise either.

Still, it must be said that he had been busy elsewhere. At sixteen he'd become the captain of the Oswestry Regiment, a local Yeomanry regiment, and two years later he transferred to the North Shropshire Yeomanry Cavalry. His full-time move to the army came after his grand tour of Europe, and he spent a year in France as a cornet in the 7th Hussars. It is unclear how much fighting he did there – his time was mostly spent drinking and gambling before he eventually resigned – but he did get promoted to major in 1822, when he came back to England.

One footnote to all this took place in the year 1819, when Mytton thought he may as well follow in his ancestors' footsteps and stand for Parliament. Not keen on the idea of campaigning for a seat, he offered prospective voters ten-pound notes (nearly £900 today) instead, and promptly became the new MP for Shrewsbury. He attended one debate in the chamber of the House of Commons for around half an hour, decided it was boring and never returned. He stood down altogether a year later, explaining that 'a proper and punctual attendance to his parliamentary duties was incompatible with his present pursuits'.

The same year, 1820, was also when his first wife Harriet Emma Jones tragically died of natural causes, a mere two years after the pair had married. Mytton married again, to Caroline Mallet Giffard the following year, but she ran away from him in 1830. Her decision was understandable; on top of having an erratic career, 'Mad Jack' Mytton, as he was nicknamed, was an all-round exhausting nightmare.

It is hard to know if every story told about him is actually true but they are all amusing, so we may as well run through them to give you an idea of what it may have been like to have shared a life with him. John Mytton liked hunting; he got his first pack of hounds as a child, and owned 700 pairs of hunting boots, 150 pairs of hunting breeches, 3,000 shirts and 1,000 hats. He didn't always use them; sometimes, when entranced by the thrill of the chase, he would tear off his clothes and ride his horse in the nude. Lord knows that must have chafed.

He also liked dogs – really, really liked them. At one point Mytton had two thousand, and would feed his favourites steak and champagne. He also had many, many horses, including his favourite, Baronet, who he allowed to walk freely in the house and who would cuddle up with him by the fire. He did try to feed one of his other horses a full bottle of port at one point, which obviously killed the poor animal.

Oh, and in 1826 he rode his horse into the Bedford Hotel in Leamington Spa, taking it up the grand staircase and onto the balcony. He then jumped over the diners in the restaurant, still seated on his horse, and out through a window onto the Parade. For a bet. That no one got hurt was a miracle, but then he didn't mind getting hurt, as he proved when he once entered his living room, then full of acquaintances, riding a trained bear. The animal behaved at first, but Mytton nicked it with a spur, causing it to attack him and then a servant. It was later put down.

We could go on but, really, you get the point – and presumably won't find it overly shocking that by 1831 Mytton had managed to spend the entirety of his enormous inheritance and fallen deeply into debt. Left with few options, he sold his estate and fled to Calais to avoid his creditors, though at least he was not alone. Having encountered a beautiful woman named Susan on Westminster Bridge, he offered her £500 a year – heaven knows where from – to leave England with him, which she agreed to do.

The move didn't dampen his eccentricity. As writer and witness to the scene Charles James Apperley (otherwise known as 'Nimrod') later recalled, Mytton once (successfully) cured some persistent hiccups by setting fire to his shirt, judging – perhaps not unfairly – that it would be the swiftest way to frighten himself. In any case, in 1833 he eventually found his way back to England where, still unable to pay his debts, he ended up in the King's Bench Prison in London. This is where he passed away the following year, not having even reached the age of forty. That he was said to have drunk eight bottles of port a day for most of his life probably explains his youthful demise, and definitely puts his behaviour into some context.

Matthew Robinson (1713–1800)

MP for Canterbury, 1747–61

Matthew Robinson was born in Horton, Kent, and went to Westminster School. He was then admitted to Lincoln's Inn in 1730, and Trinity Hall, Cambridge, in 1731, where he became a fellow four years later. In 1746 he inherited his father's estate, Mount Morris, and a year after that he became the MP for Canterbury. Records of his parliamentary career are sparse, purely because there is not much to say about it; like a lot of men from good families at the time, he was an MP and then he wasn't. Sometimes he voted and sometimes he went to his constituency, and he seemed liked enough, but that was largely that.

Being from a wealthy background, he did not need to work for money anyway, and led quite a pleasant life as a result. He split his time between London, Bath, Cambridge and Horton, and was seen as an amiable socialite wherever he went. Some of his habits were a tad odd, but were seemingly well accepted. You see, Robinson – or Lord Rokeby, as he would eventually be known – was immensely fond of water. Having spent time in the French spa town of Aix-la-Chapelle, he had taken to bathing frequently and for several hours at a time, which would be a bit excessive now but seemed deeply puzzling then.

At first, his new-found obsession drove him to swimming in the sea every day, no matter the weather, and occasionally staying in so long he would faint in the ocean and have to be picked up by his servant. The natural next step was for him to have a swimming pool built on his estate, covered by a glass roof and warmed by the sun and said to be 'probably the most comfortable bathhouse in England'. His love of water even extended to drinking it, which was not especially common at the time. He had a number of drinking fountains built on the way from Mount Morris to the seafront, and would hand out half-crown coins (a small fortune at the time) to people he saw using them, as a way to encourage the population to drink more water.

Though there were rumours about him being a cannibal and only eating raw flesh, Rokeby's diet was pretty healthy for the time. He refused to eat anything not grown in Britain, so substituted sugar for honey, would not consume wheat or coffee, which he considered too exotic, and mainly lived on boiled beef. That being said, he was a reasonable host, and though he did not host guests often at Mount Morris, full three-course meals would be served when he did. He may have been an oddball, but he was a considerate one.

His commitment to the persona also extended to his appearance, as he let his beard grow down to his knees, but at least he was in exceptional shape. Despite being of the sort of background that would easily allow him to travel around in a chaise, he insisted on doing everything he could by foot, even as he grew older. And grow older he really did: he died peacefully at the age of eighty-seven, having lived a wonderful and unique life.

Lionel Walter Rothschild (1868–1937)

MP for Aylesbury, 1899–1910

When he was seven years old, Walter Rothschild announced to his parents that he wanted to open a zoo. While a child having wild ambitions for their future is nothing out of the ordinary, young Walter had already been collecting insects and butterflies, and by the time he was ten his collection had filled his parents' shed. To be fair, the fact that his family was very wealthy and that his father was, among other things, the first ever Jewish peer meant that they had the space to accommodate their aspiring zoologist of a son. Sadly for him, though, it also meant that the Rothschilds had a fairly clear idea of how Walter's life should go, and 'lovable eccentric' was not it. Still, they did manage to find a reasonably happy balance for a while.

On the one hand, Walter got to travel to Europe and study at the University of Bonn for a year before going to Magdalen College, Oxford, then starting work at the family bank, N. M. Rothschild & Sons, at twenty-one. On the other, he was allowed to continue collecting insects and birds throughout his teenage years, storing them in rented sheds and rooms around Tring, where the family lived. For his twenty-first birthday Walter also received some land on the outskirts of Tring Park, so he could finally build his own private zoo. Three years later, in 1892, the Rothschild Museum of Zoology was opened to the public.

Sadly for Walter, his passion for animals remained something he had to do on the side for quite a while longer, as he was still working at the bank and became an MP in 1899. Not the most active of backbenchers, he spoke a grand total of five times in the Commons chamber in his eleven years on the green benches. Things finally started to look up in 1908, as he turned forty and his family allowed him to leave the bank. He then left Parliament in 1910 and could finally – finally! – pursue the one passion he had had since he was a child full-time. And pursue it he did: it is hard to even know where to start describing Rothschild's impact on zoology.

For a start, there was the scientific journal his museum started in 1894, which published over 1,700 scientific books and papers and described more than 5,000 new species of animals over the course of forty-five years. Then there was his collection – the largest ever for a private individual – which at one point counted 200,000 birds' eggs, 300,000 bird skins, 2,000 mounted mammals, 30,000 beetles, 2,000 mounted birds, 144 giant tortoises and 2 million butterflies and moths. There were also the 153 insects, 58 birds, 17 mammals, 3 spiders, 3 fish, 2 reptiles, a worm and a millipede named after him, as well as the Rothschild giraffe. Well, and there were the *Glis glis* dormice he brought back from Hungary, which escaped into the wilderness of Tring and started breeding, and which are still a localised pest in Hertfordshire to this day. Oh, and the time he decided to prove that you could tame zebras by riding a carriage drawn by several of them to Buckingham Palace.

The one hiccup came in 1932, when he had to sell off the vast majority of his expansive bird collection to the American Museum of Natural History following some money troubles he incurred after being blackmailed by a mistress. Another interesting side note comes from his Zionism and his work on the draft declaration for a Jewish homeland in Palestine. In November 1917 he received a letter from Foreign Secretary Arthur Balfour declaring government support for 'a national home for the Jewish people', which later came to be known as the Balfour Declaration. All in all, Walter Rothschild left behind quite a legacy; though attributing the building of Israel to him would be a stretch, the Natural History Museum at Tring is still standing today, all thanks to him.

John Elwes (1714–89)

MP for Berkshire, 1772–84

John Meggot was the son of a successful brewer and the grandson of an MP and a baronet. His father died when he was four years old and he inherited the family estate of

Marcham Park, in today's Oxfordshire, while his mother was left with £100,000 – just over £22 million in today's money. His youth was spent in a very predictable way, given his background; first at Westminster School, then travelling through Europe. While in Geneva he cultivated his talent for horse riding and love of hunting, and was thought to be one of the best riders on the Continent.

Though his mother was reputed to have been a frugal woman, John's life only took a turn when he started getting close to his uncle, Sudbury MP Sir Hervey Elwes, whose fortune he was hoping to inherit. Though extraordinarily wealthy, Elwes was a proud miser who only spent the equivalent of around £24,000 a year. In fact, the uncle and nephew shared a bond in railing against the extravagances of other wealthy people while sharing one glass of wine between them throughout a whole evening. Clearly keen to curry the man's favour, John Meggot even changed his name to John Elwes in 1751.

His efforts weren't in vain; in 1763 Hervey Elwes died and left his entire fortune – a whopping £50 million adjusted for inflation – to lucky, lucky John. Sadly for him, he also inherited his uncle's miserly ways and soon became known for his peculiar habits. For example, he would go to sleep as soon as it got dark outside, in order not to waste any money on candles. When at home in the colder months, he would avoid having to light several fires by going to sit with his servants. He was also said to have once worn a wig he'd found in a hedge, instead of having to purchase one himself.

In 1772 Elwes got himself elected as the MP for Berkshire after having spent a mere eighteen pence (around £30) on the election. He would ride a lean old horse to Parliament the long way round to avoid turnpike tolls, and his meals consisted of a boiled egg or piece of pancake he would keep in his pocket, occasionally for days at a time. It is unclear why he bothered going at all, as he was unattached to any party, and he did not speak in the Chamber once. Fellow MPs unsurprisingly found him to be an amusing character, and would quip that he was a politician who could never be accused of being a 'turncoat', seeing as he only owned a single suit at a time (which he also slept in, of course). Also unsurprising is the fact that he eventually stood down after twelve years, when it looked like he may have to spend some money on getting re-elected.

Still, what was especially odd about John Elwes was the inconsistency of his attitude towards his fortune. While he lived the way he did, he haemorrhaged money by endlessly lending it to acquaintances in need and refusing to ever ask for it back if they didn't repay him themselves. One notable example was the £7,000 (over £1 million) he lent to Lord Abingdon on a whim so he could place a bet on a horse race at Newmarket. He was also keen on architecture, and is one of the men whose funds made central London the way it is today – he financed Portman Square and parts of Marylebone, Baker Street and Oxford Circus. As his biographer Edward Topham put it: 'His public character lives after him pure and without stain. In private life, he was chiefly an enemy to himself . . . To others, he lent much; to himself, he denied everything.'

This was especially true of his last few years, when he became of no fixed abode and would live between the different buildings he owned which happened to be unoccupied at the time. He also started hiding small quantities of money in different places and endlessly going to check no one had found them. At death's door, a doctor came to visit him and remarked: 'with his original strength of constitution, and lifelong habits of temperance, might have lived twenty years longer, but for his continual anxiety about money'. His barrister was then instructed to draw up his will – of over £120 million today – in the firelight as lighting a candle would have been a waste.

Still, according to some, this was not quite the end of the John Elwes story. While reading about his life, you may have noticed our miserly friend bore some resemblance to one Ebenezer Scrooge from *A Christmas Carol*. This probably isn't a coincidence; though Charles Dickens was born several decades after Elwes' passing, records show that he was aware of the former MP and even made a reference to him in his last completed novel, *Our Mutual Friend*. There is no way of knowing for certain, of course, but heaven knows old Meggot could have done with a benevolent ghost or two in his time.

Charles Sibthorp (1783–1855)

MP for Lincoln, 1826–32

MP for Lincoln, 1835–55

Charles de Laet Waldo Sibthorp was one of the most famous eccentrics the House of Commons has ever seen, as hinted by the fact that even the usually dry and stony-faced parliamentary archives call him 'colourful and preposterous'.

A member of the landed gentry, he was born in Lincoln and went to study at Brasenose College, Oxford, but left before graduating in order to join the army. He served in the Royal Scots Greys, where he was promoted to lieutenant in 1806, and eventually rose to captain of the 4th Dragoon Guards. In 1822 he succeeded his brother as Lieutenant Colonel of the Royal South Lincolnshire Militia and inherited his family's estates. His first election to Parliament took place four years later when he stood for the seat of Lincoln, as was tradition in his family. This is when the fun started.

Well, nearly; on the day of the poll, someone in the crowd threw a brick at Sibthorp's head, rendering him unconscious. Still, he had given his future constituents a good idea of where he may stand on political matters when asked what he made of parliamentary reform:

On no account would I sanction any attempts to subvert that glorious fabric, our matchless Constitution, which has reached its present perfection by the experience of ages, by any new-fangled schemes which interested or deluded individuals might bring forward, and those who expect any advantages from such notions will find their visions go like a vapour and vanish into nothing.

It shouldn't have been a surprise to anyone, then, that he would turn out to be an MP so reactionary he often sounded like a parody.

In fact, he even *looked* like a parody; while fashion had long moved on, Sibthorp insisted on dressing like a Regency-era gentleman. He would walk through the Commons wearing a tall white hat, quizzing glasses on a cord, a green frock coat and white wide trousers hoisted above his top boots. Still, his stances are what really got him famous, as he was – to keep it short – against all reforms. He was against Catholic emancipation and Jewish emancipation; he was against the repeal of the Corn Laws and against the Reform Act of 1832, and the construction of the National Gallery.

One thing he was in favour of, perhaps unexpectedly, was the emancipation of slaves, which he argued for as one of the 'Saints', a group of MPs led by William Wilberforce. The role he played was an amusing one; as the debate captured the attention of the House, many parliamentarians wanted to be in the Chamber to debate the topic, but all could not always get in as there was not enough space on the benches for all MPs. Luckily, Sibthorp found a way around it, as noted in a piece of writing from the era:

> Mackintosh . . . went one day to the House of Commons at eleven in the morning to take a place. They were all taken on the benches below the gangway, and on asking the doorkeeper how they happened to be all taken so early, he said, 'Oh, sir, there is no chance of getting a place, for Colonel Sibthorp sleeps at the bawdy house close by, and comes here every morning by eight o'clock and takes places for all the Saints.'

While an admirable effort, it is also possible that he simply enjoyed having an excuse to sleep in a nearby brothel every other night. After all, 1829 was also the year his wife filed an uncontested suit for a legal separation, on account of her husband's long-running affair with Sarah Ward, a woman of 'low character'. As is tradition with politicians, he did not let inconsistencies in his personal life influence his convictions in the House. A year later he spoke against the sale of beer bill – which he thought should be named 'a bill to increase drunkenness and immorality and facilitate the sale of smuggled spirits' – as it would 'make every house in the parish not only a common drinking house, but . . . a common bawdy house'. Another highlight was his claim in 1832 that horse thieves should be 'strung up on the spot and used for dissection'.

Still, the one cause that made him famous came a bit later on, in 1839. As with all good reactionaries, Sibthorp was a dedicated royalist, but as all good reactionaries, he was also incredibly xenophobic. You can imagine, then, how he felt when it was announced that Queen Victoria was to marry the distinctly not English Prince Albert of Saxe-Coburg and Gotha. On the eve of the wedding, Parliament was set to pass a motion allowing the Consort an annuity of £50,000 p.a. Sibthorp opposed it, of course, as he thought that £30,000 was a far more reasonable sum to hand out to a mere foreigner.

Sensing an opportunity to stick it to the government, leader of the opposition Robert Peel backed the amendment, ensuring it was carried. A lesser man would have considered his victory complete, but this was not enough for the Colonel; foreigners from distant lands were not to be trusted, and he kept an eye on the Prince Consort. When Albert started working on the Great Exhibition, due to take place in 1851 in the purpose-built Crystal Palace in Hyde Park, Sibthorp knew what to do.

In the Chamber he called on God – no less – to send 'a heavy hailstorm' to destroy 'that fraud upon the public called . . . the "Crystal Palace" – that accursed building, erected to encourage the foreigner at the expense of the already grievously distressed English artisan'. He also called it 'one of the greatest humbugs, one of the greatest frauds, one of the greatest absurdities ever known', and would refer to Crystal Palace as a 'palace of tomfoolery'. When his efforts to stop the exhibition going ahead failed, he made it clear that 'for his own part, he would not for a thousand guineas enter the walls or approach within smell of the unwieldy, ill-devised, and unwholesome Castle of Glass'. In short: not a fan.

Thankfully for Britain, his prediction that foreigners would use a visit to the Great Exhibition as an excuse to learn of the country's defences, and then attack it once it was weak and open, didn't come to pass. Sadly for him, Queen Victoria very much noted his campaigning – as well as his previous work against her husband – and made her feelings for the MP known the year the exhibition took place. When the royal family travelled up to Scotland by train, their route took them through Lincoln, which had been decorated for a royal visit. Though the royal train did stop in the city, the queen did not alight; the reasoning behind the snub was never made public, but was widely assumed to be a dig towards Sibthorp.

Not that it would have really mattered to him; on top of being against, well, practically everything else, the Colonel also hated trains, which he deemed to be a 'degrading form of transport' and would call the 'steam humbug'. He (unsurprisingly) longed for the happy days of 'travelling the turnpike roads in chaises, carriages and stages', and thought railways were a fad. In order to try and convince his fellow parliamentarians, he would closely read local papers to collect stories of train accidents and would then accuse railway companies of downplaying them, suppressing the gorier details and lying about the number of casualties. That he believed the press in general to be untrustworthy and government propaganda should go without saying.

Though he did start taking trains himself towards the end of his life, it did not dampen his hatred of them, and one of his crowning achievements was to prevent the Great Northern Railway from extending its line through Lincoln. That did not stop him from remaining the city's MP until his death. In fact, his constituents had, some years earlier, bought him a diamond ring inscribed with the words 'The ornament and reward of integrity presented to Charles de Laet Waldo Sibthorp by the grateful people of Lincoln'. Another view was taken by Charles Dickens, who wrote that Colonel Sibthorp was 'the most amusing person in the House. Can anything be more exquisitely absurd than the burlesque grandeur of his air, as he strides up the lobby, his eyes rolling like those of a Turk's head in a cheap Dutch clock? He is generally harmless, though, and always amusing.' That's more like it.

John Wilkes (1725–97)

MP for Aylesbury, 1757–64

MP for Middlesex, 1768–9

MP for Middlesex, 1774–90

There is a lot to say about John Wilkes, and indeed a lot has been written about him over the past few centuries. He is, after all, a major figure in British political history, and someone who achieved a lot. For this reason, what follows will largely focus on the more amusing parts of his time in and around Parliament; if you wish to find out more about the serious stuff, there are many biographies out there which will do the job just fine.

So, keeping this in mind: the son of a successful malt distiller, John Wilkes was born in Clerkenwell, London, and went to boarding school before being privately tutored. By fourteen he had mastered Greek and Latin, and at eighteen he went to study at the University of Leiden in the Netherlands, which he briefly left in 1745 to fight in a Loyal Association during the Jacobite rebellion. He came back to Britain for good in 1747 to get married to Mary Mead, who was ten years older than him but gave him the manor of Aylesbury in Buckinghamshire. Wilkes was elected a Fellow of the Royal Society two years later, but more importantly, became a member of the Hellfire Club around that time.

Also nicknamed the Medmenham Monks and the Knights of St Francis of Wycombe, the group brought together high society men wishing to behave appallingly. This iteration of the club had been launched by Sir Francis Dashwood, and its motto was '*Fais ce que tu voudras*' ('Do what thou wilt'). In practice, this meant excessive drinking, excessive eating and 'obscene parodies of religious rites', alongside the odd (alleged) prostitute and black mass. Far from being a wall-flower at these gatherings, Wilkes was rumoured to have once brought a baboon wearing a cape and horns to one of the club's mock rituals.

Presumably getting bored of being 'a rake and libertine in the usual manner of the juvenile wealthy of his day', he decided to stand for Parliament in 1754 but lost, despite having bribed a captain to land a shipload of opposition voters from London in Norway instead of at Berwick-upon-Tweed, which was the seat he coveted. Undeterred, he stood again in Aylesbury in 1757, bribed many of his prospective voters, and won.

His parliamentary beginnings weren't especially fruitful. According to a contemporary, 'he seem[ed] to have had no other idea than to play the political game as it was played by all young gentlemen of ability and means'. Harold Walpole, meanwhile, said of his maiden speech that 'he spoke coldly and insipidly, though with impertinence; his manner was poor, and his countenance horrid'. Still, he clearly enjoyed life in the Commons to some extent, as in 1761 he gave five pounds to three hundred of the five hundred voters in Aylesbury in order to retain his seat.

His personality also made him popular. Though he was said to be the ugliest man in England at the time, because of a heavy squint and protruding jaw, this didn't seem to bother him too much; he was a successful womaniser and would quip that it took him only half an hour to 'talk away his face'. He was also famously witty: when a constituent informed him that he'd rather vote for the devil, Wilkes shot back 'Naturally – and if your friend decides against standing, can I count on your vote?'

But Wilkes wasn't just an amusing man, and though the early years of his parliamentary career weren't particularly driven by convictions, everything changed in 1762 when the new king, George III, had his friend the Earl of Bute installed as prime minister. Bute was largely seen as incompetent by the Commons, and Wilkes decided to make his dislike known. In June that year he launched a newspaper, the *North*

Briton, a title blatantly meant to mock the *Briton*, a pro-government newspaper, as well as annoy the new Scottish prime minister. In its first issue he wrote that 'the liberty of the press is the birthright of a Briton, and is justly esteemed the firmest bulwark of the liberties of this country', and he soon started testing the very limits of said free press. After the King's Speech at the opening of Parliament a year later, he wrote that George III had given 'his sacred name to the most odious measures and the most unjustifiable public declarations from a throne ever renowned for truth, honour and the unsullied virtue'. Mince his words he did not.

It got him in trouble from the very first year it was launched. In 1762, Bute supporter William Talbot challenged Wilkes to a duel after being mocked by him in the *North Briton*. Luckily neither party was hurt in the process, and the pair went off to share a bottle of claret at a nearby inn. This was a warning Wilkes should have heeded, but predictably he did not change course, as we know from the excoriating piece he wrote about King George's speech.

Then prime minister George Grenville had not taken kindly to it, and neither had the king. As a result, general warrants were issued for the arrest of John Wilkes and his associates for the publication of a 'seditious and treasonable paper', and forty-eight people were initially seized in a quest for evidence before Wilkes was arrested and thrown into the Tower of London. Luckily for him, he appeared in court a week later and argued that parliamentary privilege meant he could not be arrested for libel, which the judge agreed with. Freed, he then sued the Earl of Halifax, the secretary of state who'd been responsible for the arrest, and his underlings for trespass, and won. Clearly drunk on his own cockiness by that point, he was asked by a French acquaintance about the limits of the freedom of the press in England, and responded 'I cannot tell, but I am trying to find out'.

Sadly for him, it was all about to go downhill from there. In 1763, Samuel Martin, a supporter of the king, challenged Wilkes to a duel after Wilkes called him 'the most treacherous, base, selfish, mean, abject, low-lived and dirty fellow that ever wriggled himself into a secretaryship' in the *North Briton*. A good shot, Martin managed to get Wilkes in the stomach, leaving him seriously wounded though alive. Only a week later, Parliament voted to establish that parliamentary privilege could not protect MPs from charges of seditious libel, which showed that the Commons hadn't been on his side in this fight.

Then things got worse. The same month, Lord Sandwich, by then a secretary of state, read out 'An Essay on Woman' to the House of Lords, in an effort to oust Wilkes from Parliament for good. The erotic poem had been written by Wilkes and his acquaintance Thomas Potter around ten years earlier, intending it to be an obscene parody of Alexander Pope's 'An Essay on Man', and was dedicated to famous courtesan Fanny Murray. Here's an extract:

> *Passions, like elements, though born to fight,*
> *By female pow'r subdu'd, are alter'd quite;*
> *These 'tis enough to temper and employ,*
> *While what affords most pleasure, can destroy.*
>
> *All spread their charms, but charm not all alike,*
> *On different senses different objects strike;*
> *Hence different ladies, more or less inflame;*

Or different pow'rs sometimes attend the fame;
And calling up each passion of the breast,
Each lady, in her turn, subdues the rest.

As a side note, Lord Sandwich had been a lover of Murray's and a fellow Hellfire Club member, though it was rumoured that he'd been seeking revenge ever since Wilkes had scared the living hell out of him by leaping out in front of him during a drunken seance. In any case, the government wanted to be rid of the thorn in its side, and did what it had to do. Though the poem had never been officially published and only a dozen copies of it existed, presumably because they'd been meant for Hellfire members, the plan worked. The poem was voted by the Lords to be libel and a breach of privilege, and they also declared the old issue of the *North Briton* to be seditious libel.

Nursing his wounds, Wilkes fled the country and travelled to Paris. This was a wise decision, as in January 1764 the government carried a motion for his expulsion from the House of Commons, and he was tried *in absentia* and found guilty of publishing a seditious libel and an obscene and impious libel. Left with few other options, Wilkes decided to wait it out in Paris until a government closer to his own convictions got in power, but in vain. By 1768 he found himself in trouble with his French creditors so decided to go big and go home, returning to Britain and standing as an MP on a platform of public liberty and opposition to the government.

Worried that throwing him in jail would only make him more popular, the government held back on his arrest, something they probably lived to regret. Though he didn't manage to win in London, he did get a seat in Middlesex, after which he was immediately arrested and taken to King's Bench Prison. As the government had feared, large crowds soon started to assemble by the prison calling for Wilkes's release; worried that a mob would try to physically get him out, troops opened fire, killing seven people, which predictably only made the protesters angrier. Around a month later, Wilkes was found guilty of libel and given twenty-two months in prison and a £1,000 fine.

What followed was a somewhat comical game of parliamentary hokey-cokey. In February 1769, John Wilkes was expelled from Parliament because he had been an outlaw when he'd returned. Later that month he stood in Middlesex again and won, but was expelled again. In March there was a by-election, which he won before getting expelled. Then, in April, he was elected once more, and expelled one last time, by which point Parliament made the controversial move of declaring his opponent, Henry Luttrell, the new MP for Middlesex.

This didn't put an end to Wilkes's ambitions. Later that year he became an alderman of London, then was released from prison in April 1770 and became a sheriff in 1771. He tormented Parliament once more that year, when it tried to prevent newspapers from publishing reports on what took place in the House of Commons. Wilkes challenged the move, and although the government initially got two of his printers arrested in retaliation, a mob grew outside Parliament and forced it to climb down.

Three years later he became Mayor of London and was (finally) elected MP for Middlesex again. This is where we will leave it: though John Wilkes had a lot of life left in him by that point, there isn't much of interest to us in his later days, and we must move on to others. Still, what a character he was.

George Sitwell (1860–1943)

MP for Scarborough, 1885–6

MP for Scarborough, 1892–5

George Reresby Sitwell was the fourth Baronet Sitwell, but sadly, and unlike the first Baronet Sitwell who we will encounter later, he was not so good they named him twice. Born in London, he inherited the family's title at the age of two when his father died, and took it in his stride. It was said that a few years later he met someone on a train and declared: 'I am Sir George Sitwell, baronet. I am four years old and the youngest baronet in England.'

Educated at Eton (of course) then Christ Church, Oxford (where else?), he briefly was a lieutenant in the West Yorkshire Yeoman Cavalry before deciding to run for Parliament in his early twenties. He became the MP for Scarborough in 1885, but lost the seat a year later; he gained it again in 1892, then lost it once more in 1895, and gave up on politics after that.

Instead, he decided to live a fairly pleasant life in Renishaw Hall, the family seat, which had been abandoned and which he set out to refurbish. To give you an idea of the sort of man Sitwell was, a note at the entrance to the country house read: 'I must ask anyone entering the house never to contradict me in any way, as it interferes with the functioning of the gastric juices and prevents my sleeping at night'.

In fairness to him, his personal life was not very happy. He had married Ida Emily Augusta Denison in 1886, and her first act as his wife had been to try to run away from him; she soon turned to champagne, whisky and spending her husband's money as her main hobbies. The couple had three children together, but were – perhaps unsurprisingly – not the best of parents.

As his daughter Edith Sitwell later wrote, 'I was unpopular with my parents from the moment of my birth and throughout my childhood and youth'. It probably did not help that Edith grew up to be a novelist, given her father was convinced that too much writing was a danger to one's physical health, for reasons that remain unclear. Not limiting himself to embarrassing his daughter, Sitwell also went through a phase of trying (and failing) to pay for his son Sacheverell's Eton fees with produce grown on the family's grounds.

George's real passion was . . . well, trivial things. He wrote a number of (unpublished) books on topics ranging from 'Pig Keeping in the Thirteeenth Century' to the history of the fork, and came up with a number of wonderfully useless inventions. Among other things, he thought of a musical toothbrush that played 'Annie Laurie' and a miniature gun for shooting wasps.

Sitwell took his inventions very seriously. One of his favourites was the 'Sitwell egg', comprised of a 'yolk' of smoked meat and an 'egg white' of rice wrapped in a synthetic 'shell'. Convinced it would be the ideal snack for travellers, he went to meet Gordon Selfridge to try and get him to sell it at his Oxford Street shop, announcing himself with a wonderful 'I am Sir George Sitwell and I've brought my egg with me'. Needless to say, Selfridge's did not purchase the Sitwell egg.

One lifelong and comparatively successful love of the baronet's was landscaping. Very fond of Italian designs, he toured the country studying the local gardening, and later published the (somewhat) acclaimed *On the Making of Gardens*. Still, his eccentricity followed him wherever he went, as whenever he travelled he would intentionally mislabel all his (self-)medication, lest someone tried to steal it for themselves.

He even took his fondness for garden design too far, once trying to stencil blue willow patterns on the white cows on his estate – the animals did not co-operate. In any case, the last few years of his life were sombre ones, as his wife's increasingly erratic behaviour landed her in court in 1915, then in Holloway Prison for three months after she was convicted of fraud.

By that point Sitwell had already retired into his own little world where, among other things, he forbade people from using electricity in the house. In 1925 he handed Renishaw over to his son and retired to Italy, where he lived until his death. When his wife passed away in 1937, his valet remarked 'At least Sir George will know where Her Ladyship spends her afternoons'.

Years after his father's death, Osbert Sitwell published *Tales My Father Taught Me*, in which he wrote of George: 'He was adept at taking hold of the wrong end of a thousand sticks, yet when by chance he seized the right end, his grasp of it was remarkable because of the intellectual power and application, as well as the learning, which he brought to his task.'

2

The Unfortunate

An instant previous he was in the full possession of health and spirits, he now lay bleeding and mangled before his friends!

Manchester Guardian, *18 September 1830, the day William Huskisson died*

Matthew Browne (1563–1603)

MP for Gatton, 1601

Sir Matthew Browne of Betchworth Castle was never famous, but he pops up in a few interesting corners of history. After studying at Magdalen College in Oxford, he joined the Inner Temple, where he met a fellow named Nicholas Brend. Browne served as a member of Charles Howard's expedition to Spain in 1596, which led to the Capture of Cádiz, an important victory in the Anglo-Spanish War. There, he was knighted by the Earl of Essex, Robert Devereux.

In 1600, Browne was appointed deputy lieutenant of Surrey, then in 1601 was elected MP for the rotten borough of Gatton. Later that year he helped Brend, who owned the land on which the Globe theatre was first built in 1599, with some financial and legal transactions to help him keep the property in the family when he died. Still, none of this is why we're here now.

Browne deserves a mention because in 1603 he fought a duel on horseback against John Townshend MP in Hounslow Heath. We know it was started by a 'quarrel' – which is presumably not unusual for a duel – but no one thought to record what the quarrel was about. In any case, he died on the spot.

John Townshend (1568–1603)

MP for Castle Rising, 1593

MP for Norfolk, 1597

MP for Orford, 1601

Sir John Townshend of Raynham Hall started life in much the same way as Matthew Browne. Educated at Magdalen College in Oxford, he served in the English army in the Netherlands before taking part in the expedition to Cádiz, where he was knighted as well.

In 1600 a feud with Sir Christopher Heydon, another MP, very nearly led to a duel, but the pair were summoned by the Privy Council and forced to put an end to it. That same year, he did manage to duel against Theophilus Finch, who would later become an MP as well, over 'a point of honour', demonstrating either his bad temper, taste for the blade, or a combination of both.

It is perhaps unsurprising, then, that in 1601 he found himself on horseback on Hounslow Heath, duelling against Matthew Browne. While the latter died during the fight, Townshend succumbed to his wounds a day later, making the whole affair look rather silly. Or, to misquote Oscar Wilde: to lose one MP in a duel may be regarded as a misfortune; to lose both looks like carelessness.

Arthur Crosfield (1865–1938)

MP for Warrington, 1906–10

A soap magnate and Liberal politician, Arthur Crosfield is mostly known for having bought Parkfield, a house in Highgate, and turning it into Witanhurst. By the time he was done, it had become the second largest private residence in London after Buckingham Palace.* Witanhurst had a ballroom, a glass rotunda, twenty-five bedrooms and four tennis courts (Crosfield and his wife would host an annual tournament, including several players who had just competed at Wimbledon).

He was an active parliamentarian, speaking fairly frequently in the Chamber, and made a lovely plea for the light-hearted in his maiden speech:

> The allusion has been made in this debate – and indeed the Prime Minister laid emphasis on the fact – that in their graver issues politics are something much more serious than a game. Yes, that is true, and so is life, but as the right hon. Gentleman the Member for Montrose has reminded us, laughter has a forepart in it.
>
> It would indeed be hard luck to deprive the poor politician of his little bit of humour. I am told that one day [actor and comedian] Dan Leno came down to the House, and the hon. Gentleman the Member for Woolwich – whose wit and genius are not second even

* It was later owned by the family of Bashar al-Assad, and was where the BBC filmed *Fame Academy*, so fair to say it has had an eventful history.

to Leno's – met him when he was leaving, and said, 'Well, Dan, what do you think of it all?' 'Not bad,' said Leno. 'Not bad; but I think it would go better to the piano.'

He lost his seat in the election of 1910 and was made a baronet five years later. Among other things, he was a very successful golf player (and the 1905 amateur golf champion of France), a piano composer, the chairman of the National Playing Fields Association and a governor of Highgate School.

Sadly, things went downhill for Crosfield in the mid 1930s, when he got involved in a Greek mining venture – his wife was the daughter of a Greek merchant – and lost most of his fortune.

In 1938 he was travelling on the Geneva–Ventimiglia Express when he managed to fall out of the window of the train. Managing to make him sound like a beloved family Labrador, the *Manchester Guardian* noted a week later that 'Sir Arthur was always very fond of fresh air and liked open windows'.

James Tomkinson (1840–1910)

MP for Crewe, 1900–10

The story of James Tomkinson is really the story of the House of Commons Steeplechase. The horse race between MPs was inaugurated in 1889, the first event taking place in Buckinghamshire: it involved a special train bringing the members of Parliament and other interested parties to Hillesden.

The race was such a success that it became an annual

event, prompting Conservative magazine *Judy* to publish this poem in 1890:

> *Not Quite Point to Pointless!*
> *A meeting gay, the other day*
> *(Last Saturday, to be exact),*
> *Drew many down to Rugby town*
> *(Somewhere in Warwickshire, in fact),*
> *And there, one reads, were gallant steeds*
> *And riders (as is oft the case)*
> *To ride, d'ye see ('twixt you and me),*
> *The House of Commons Steeplechase!*

After a five-year hiatus, the race intermittently came back in 1897, 1898 and 1907, then in 1910. This is where Tomkinson comes in; he was, by the time the last steeple-chase took place, nearly seventy years old, a Liberal MP and a member of the Privy Council. He had sustained serious injuries riding in the past (including a broken collarbone), but they clearly did not stop him from wanting to take part.

They probably should have. As the race started, he fell off his mare head first, fractured his spine and died the next day – and that was the end of the House of Commons Steeplechase.

Thomas Robinson (1608–65)

MP for Helston, 1660–5

A reasonably active though fairly uninteresting member of Parliament, Thomas Robinson was gored to death by a pet bull. Some years later, an old woman was tried for having bewitched the bull, since clearly it had to be a woman's fault and not, say, a predictable consequence of keeping a bull as a pet.

John Whitson (1554–1629)

MP for Bristol, 1605–21

MP for Bristol, 1625–8

John Whitson was an interesting character. Born and educated in the Forest of Dean, he moved to Bristol to find work and was taken under the wing of Nicholas Cutt, a rich vintner and member of the Society of Merchant Venturers. When Cutt died in 1582, Whitson got together with his wife – or more specifically, was rumoured to have seduced her in a wine cellar, which simultaneously gives us too much information yet not quite enough – and the pair married soon after.

Whitson eventually became a very successful merchant and lord mayor of Bristol, before going to represent the city in Parliament. He was active in Holland, Germany, France, Ireland and several Mediterranean countries, trading in leather, lead, iron and cloth, and buying currants, wine, oil and alum in return.

Though he seemingly was a controversial figure at the time (or at least one adept at making enemies), he did hand out a lot of his wealth to those who needed it, including £500 – over £130,000 in today's money – to a number of young merchants, handicraft tradesmen and freemen of Bristol in 1627.

In a staggering show of bad luck, a year later Whitson fell off his horse outside a blacksmith's and landed head first on an upturned nail. A large portion of his estate was left to charity, as requested in his will.

Most notably, he left £90 per annum from the manor of Burnett, which he owned, to provide a home and eight years of education in English and sewing to 'forty poor women children', who would wear red outfits to match those of the boys attending Queen Elizabeth's Hospital school.

This turned out to be the founding of Redmaids' High School, the oldest girls' school in England. Every year, Redmaids' High School Founders' Commemoration Day now takes place, not on the day of Whitson's death but on the day when a man stabbed him in the face but he survived, making his stupid demise two years after that even more poignant.

Spencer Perceval (1762–1812)

MP for Northampton, 1796–1812

The seventh son of John Perceval, the second Earl of Egmont and an adviser to the Prince of Wales, Spencer Perceval came from a distinguished family but was too far down the line to get anywhere near his father's lands or titles.

Instead he became a barrister and moved into a house with his brother, and soon the pair fell in love with two sisters. The father of the women agreed to one union but thought Spencer was, to put it bluntly, too poor to get his daughter. Undeterred, the pair soon eloped to the glamorous and distant lands of East Grinstead in Sussex, moved into a flat above a carpet shop, and eventually had thirteen children together.

After managing to become a King's Counsel at thirty-three – one of the youngest ever – Perceval joined the Commons that same year, replacing his cousin who'd received his father's earldom and moved up to the House of Lords.

An able speaker, he rose through the ranks quickly. After five years on the green benches, he became Henry Addington's solicitor general in 1801 then his attorney general a year later, staying on under William Pitt the Younger. When Pitt died and was replaced by Lord Grenville, Perceval became leader of the Pittite opposition and used the time to defend Princess Caroline against the Prince of Wales, after he accused her of having an illegitimate child. The inquiry found her innocent but King George III still didn't want her back in court, although that didn't matter for long. After Grenville's ministry fell, Perceval joined the government again under the Duke of Portland, and used the opportunity to formally acquit her on all charges and recommend that she return to court.

By that point he had become Chancellor of the Exchequer, following a valiant but ultimately unsuccessful attempt to claim he didn't know enough about financial affairs (because he wanted to be Home Secretary instead). A decent enough chancellor in the end, he found himself the ideal – or, well, least contentious – candidate to become prime minister when Portland resigned after having had a stroke.

In an amusing twist of fate, Perceval then asked five

different politicians to be his chancellor and all five turned him down, forcing him to keep the damn job he never wanted in the first place. This was not the last of his problems: given that most of his cabinet belonged in the House of Lords, he at one point only had one other cabinet minister with him in the Commons, which unsurprisingly weakened his every move.

Still, he managed to cling on for a very reasonable (and increasingly impressive) two and a half years, until 11 May 1812. As Spencer Perceval walked into the lobby of the House of Commons that evening, he was shot in the chest. He was immediately moved to a nearby room but by the time a surgeon arrived, his heart had stopped.

An inquest was held the next day at the Cat and Bagpipes pub near Downing Street, which frankly doesn't feel like a place conveying the level of gravity you'd associate with the brutal killing of a serving prime minister, but a verdict of wilful murder was returned nonetheless.

The murderer, John Bellingham, was a merchant broker who had once found himself imprisoned in Russia while working there as an export representative. Convinced he deserved compensation from the government for what had happened to him, he'd originally wanted to kill the British ambassador to Russia, but had settled on poor old Spencer instead.

Now mostly remembered for his tragic death, Perceval really was a perfectly decent prime minister, as remarked in a poem published in 1812:

> *Such was his private, such his public life,*
> *That all who differ'd in polemic strife,*

Or varied in opinion with his plan,
Agreed with one accord to love the man.

Similarly, his fellow MP John Ward, who went on to become Foreign Secretary, dryly noted: 'His talents were admirable, and if he had not been a lawyer he would probably have risen to the character of a great man . . . Nothing could be so gentlemanlike and fair as his management of the House of Commons'.

As for John Bellingham – he unsurprisingly hanged for his crime, but one of his descendants, Henry Bellingham, became an MP in 1983 and, in 1997, lost his seat to one Roger Percival described – despite the slight difference of spelling in the surname – as a direct descendant of Spencer Perceval, in what the press portrayed as dynastic revenge. He joined the Commons again in 2001 and in 2012, and laid some flowers at a ceremony marking two hundred years since Perceval's murder, which feels like a neat way to end the whole thing.

James Mackintosh (1765–1832)

MP for Nairn, 1813–18

James Mackintosh led a remarkable life. Descended from old Highland families, he grew up near Inverness, and by thirteen was convincing his friends to do pretend debates modelled on the House of Commons. He studied medicine at Edinburgh University, then moved to London in 1788, where he became one of the co-founders of what would later become the RSPCA. Fascinated by what was happening over the Channel, he wrote *Vindiciae Gallicae: A Defence of the French Revolution and its English Admirers* in 1791, which was soon seen as one of the main pieces of writing on the topic, inspiring the poet Thomas Campbell to call him 'the apostle of liberalism'.

Buoyed by the popularity of his book, he abandoned medicine to become a lawyer, and soon became famous both for the lectures he delivered at Lincoln's Inn and for his defence of Jean-Gabriel Peltier against Napoleon. (Peltier had become a refugee in England when the Terror started in France, and got in trouble with the head of state when he called for his assassination; though the jury found him guilty in the end, Mackintosh's speech and its French trans-lation were widely read across Europe.)

It didn't take long for him to move on, and by 1804 he was living in India and was the chief judge of Bombay. In his spare time he founded the Bombay Literary Society, a predecessor to the Asiatic Society of Mumbai that still exists today.

Mackintosh came back to Britain in 1811 and entered Parliament two years later as a Whig. According to contem-poraries, his time there was mixed. On the one hand fellow MP James Scarlett called him 'the ablest speaker in the House of Commons' while on the other Whig lawyer James Tosh called him 'mild, liberal and with just and enlarged views on almost every subject; but without much dignity or firm-ness of mind. Indeed he has several times lamented his want of firmness and resolution'.

In any case, politics was never his sole interest. While an MP he also taught law and politics and wrote a number of philosophical essays and historical books. It is unclear, looking back now, whether Mackintosh was a one-of-a-kind polymath or simply a man with a short attention span who spread himself too thin. Perhaps he was both: according to writer Sydney Smith, 'his conversation was more brilliant than that of any human being I ever had the good fortune to be acquainted with' but he 'was utterly unfit for the business of life'.

Still, what we do know is that all his pursuits and interests came to an abrupt end in 1832, when he choked on a chicken bone while having dinner in the House of Commons. He swallowed it and was given medicine to throw it back up, which brought out, according to him, 'one of the largest pieces of flesh and bone which has been commonly removed from a living gullet'. Though he wrote after the incident that he was already feeling better, the wound in his throat got infected and killed him under a month later.

William Payne-Gallwey (1807–81)

MP for Thirsk, 1851–80

It is well known that quantity does not equal quality, and William Payne-Gallwey's parliamentary career rather proves it. Despite spending thirty years in the House of Commons, his local paper, the *Northern Echo*, lamented that 'although he has heard the burning words of Mr Gladstone, the polished satire of Mr Disraeli, the sustained eloquence of John Bright, and the incisive epigrams of Mr Lowe, he has never acquired the art of public speaking'.

Still, there are many ways to gain notoriety, and Payne-Gallwey managed it a year after he stood down as an MP, when he tripped and fell on a turnip, then died from the injury.

Edward Legge (1710–47)

MP for Portsmouth, 1747

The son of the first Earl of Dartmouth, Edward Legge did what any young man from a good family did in those days and joined the Navy at sixteen. He quickly rose through the ranks and was a captain at twenty-eight, ending up in the West Indies as commodore in 1747. As it happened, the parliamentary seat of Portsmouth was going spare that year, and the duke who controlled the area nominated Legge for it.

Despite being on the other side of the world during the campaign, Legge was duly elected unopposed. Somewhat awkwardly, his family found out four days later that Edward had, by that point, been dead for three months, making him the MP returned the longest time after his death even to this day. You win some, you lose some.

James Wriothesley (1605–24)

MP for Callington, 1621–2

MP for Winchester, 1624

If you worry you did not achieve enough when you were young, it is perhaps best you look away now. The godson of

James I of England, James Wriothesley was made a Knight of the Bath at the age of eleven and first elected to the Commons at fifteen.

Though practically still a child, he took part in several committees in Parliament, and was a reasonably active MP. In 1624 he was made captain in an English regiment and went to fight in the Eighty Years' War, but died from a fever in the Netherlands. He was nineteen.

Alfred Dobbs (1882–1945)

MP for Smethwick, 1945

There's bad luck and then there's being Alfred Dobbs. A community stalwart in Leeds, he was elected to the executive committee of the National Union of Boot and Shoe Operatives, then became a city councillor, an alderman, a magistrate and eventually the leader of the Labour group and chairman of the Housing Committee on Leeds City Council.

Despite being a member of Labour's National Executive Committee for several years and the chair of the Labour Party for two years, he struggled to win a seat. He stood in Altrincham in 1929 and Leeds North East in 1931 and 1935, but lost all three times.

Finally, in 1945, he stood in Smethwick and won. The very next day he swerved his car to avoid a child, crashed into a military vehicle and was killed.

Robert Aglionby Slaney (1791–1862)

MP for Shrewsbury, 1826–34

MP for Shrewsbury, 1837–41

MP for Shrewsbury, 1847–52

MP for Shrewsbury, 1857–62

Robert Slaney was a busy and worldly man. Before standing for election he was a barrister, wrote pamphlets, travelled around Europe, learned Italian and French and was interested in agriculture, mechanics and economics. In his spare time he was also an able sportsman who went shooting, played cricket for several teams and rode his own horses in the Shrewsbury races.

What followed was a game of musical chairs between him and his constituents as neither could really decide whether he should be the MP for Shrewsbury; sometimes they voted him out, sometimes he didn't stand, but he did always come back eventually.

He was known in Parliament for his tireless efforts to improve matters for the poor, from arguing for more education to access to better work, and helped set up the Select Committee on Public Health.

On 1 May 1862, Slaney attended the opening of the London International Exhibition and hurt his leg when he fell through a gap in a platform floor. Clearly thinking nothing of it, he kept touring the exhibition, and attended Parliament the following day. Sadly, gangrene set in, and he was dead by the end of the month.

Guy Cuthbert Dawnay (1848–89)

MP for North Riding of Yorkshire, 1882–5

We do not know much about Guy Dawnay. We know that his upbringing was as banal as it can be for a man of a certain background – Eton, Oxford – that he was an unremarkable MP, and that after losing his seat he served as Lord Salisbury's Surveyor General of the Ordnance, which is hardly thrilling.

Still, we also know that he enjoyed going to Africa to hunt, and that on a trip to modern-day Kenya he was killed by a buffalo.

William Huskisson (1770–1830)

MP for Morpeth, 1796–1800

MP for Morpeth, 1801–2

MP for Liskeard, 1804–7

MP for Harwich, 1807–12

MP for Chichester, 1812–23

MP for Liverpool, 1823–30

Born in Worcestershire, William Huskisson was sent off to France in 1783 to live with his great-uncle, who worked for the British Embassy. By the time he came back to England in his early twenties, he was fluent in French and had a keen interest in politics, having witnessed the French Revolution from up close.

He was soon noticed by William Pitt the Younger, then prime minister, and his Home Secretary Henry Dundas, and was made Under-Secretary at War by 1795. As was common at the time, he took a break from politics in 1801, before coming back to Parliament two years later and assuming various front-bench positions, from Secretary to the Treasury to Leader of the House of Commons.

Though he is now mostly known for his free trade advocacy and dedication to Liverpool, he was also a pro-planters Secretary of State for War and the Colonies, and ignored pleas to introduce a minimum wage when he was president of the Board of Trade, so – swings and roundabouts.

In any case, what he is most famous for has nothing to do with politics but instead took place at the opening of the Liverpool and Manchester Railway on 15 September 1830. Huskisson had recently had surgery on his kidneys and been instructed by his doctor to take some rest, but he did not want to miss the event.

He and other dignified guests rode on a special train built for the Duke of Wellington, one of the eight put on the tracks that day. The locomotives stopped at Parkside station, roughly halfway between the two cities, for a short break.

Despite having been told not to leave the train, a number of people did exactly that, including Huskisson. Another train started approaching on the other line, and passengers were told to be careful. Most climbed back to their seats or walked out of the way, but famously clumsy Huskisson panicked, crossed the track, changed his mind, and crossed it again.

He tried to clamber back into his carriage but the door hadn't been latched; the train arrived, and he was pushed onto the tracks, where his leg got mangled. Once the locomotive had passed, people rushed to his side, at which point Huskisson (not unreasonably) cried out 'This is the death of me!'

Leg in a makeshift tourniquet and his wife and three doctors by his side, Huskisson was loaded onto the Duke's train, which was relieved of several carriages. Because word of the news had yet to travel, people were standing by the side of the tracks on the way to Manchester, cheering and waving, and because the carriages were so light, the train broke world speed records by reaching almost forty miles per hour.

The party stopped in Eccles to go to the house of the town's vicar. Aside from other concerns, such injuries were still unheard of in 1830, prompting surgeon Joseph Brandreth to later write of the incident:

> It is a perfect mystery how the wound was produced . . . The leg half way between the knee and ankle was almost entirely severed, except a small portion on the outside, but the boot was scarcely marked at all. Half-way but rather higher up between the knee and body, the whole flesh was torn off above the bones broken, but the artery which lies over and above it was not injured; which accounts for the small quantities of blood lost. The flesh on the outward and lower side was not injured much.

Despite Huskisson remaining conscious, it was eventually agreed that the leg had to be amputated for him to survive, but that he was too weak to survive major surgery. Resigned to his fate, William Huskisson amended his will to ensure his wife would inherit all his property, received the sacrament, and had drawn his last breath by the evening.

Dingle Foot (1905–78)

MP for Dundee, 1931–45

MP for Ipswich, 1957–70

Dingle Foot's life started and ended poorly. It started poorly because his parents named him Dingle Foot, which hopefully for him didn't sound as funny then as it does now.

Still, it didn't stop him from becoming president of the Oxford Union, getting called to the Bar, and practising as a solicitor in, among other places, Ghana, Nigeria, Sierra Leone, Malaysia, Pakistan and Bahrain.

A Liberal MP in his first act in Parliament, he joined Winston Churchill's wartime coalition as a parliamentary secretary, and was on the delegation to the San Francisco Conference that resulted in the Charter of the United Nations being drawn up.

After losing his seat in 1945 and failing to gain another one, he spent time as the moderator of *In the News*, a BBC current affairs show, where he was often joined by his brother Michael Foot, the future leader of the opposition. Foot left the Liberals for the Labour Party in 1957 and joined Parliament again that year, then became Harold Wilson's solicitor general and joined the Privy Council.

All in all, he was an accomplished man with a respected

career, which makes it all the sadder that he choked to death on a bone in a chicken sandwich in Hong Kong.

Arthur Clinton (1840–70)

MP for Newark, 1865–8

It feels a bit trite to describe someone as having lived fast and died young, but there isn't really any other way to describe the existence of Lord Arthur Clinton. The son of a duke, he had an eventful childhood. His parents divorced after his mother eloped with her lover, Conservative peer Horatio Walpole, with whom she had an illegitimate son also named Horatio.

He joined the Royal Navy at fourteen and went to fight in the Crimean War that very same year. Three years later he was in the Naval Brigade and took part in the capture of Lucknow during the Indian Mutiny. By twenty-one he was a lieutenant.

At twenty-five he stood for Parliament in Newark, where he replaced his brother. After three unremarkable years in the Commons, he was declared bankrupt – with debts of over £6 million in today's money – and stood down in 1868.

At some point around then, he started living with Ernest Boulton, who had been dressing as a woman since childhood and went by the name of Stella. On 28 April 1870 Boulton and fellow cross-dresser Frederick Park were arrested on suspicion of practising anal sex, and were charged with 'conspiring and inciting persons to commit an unnatural offence', along with several other men including Clinton.

The news drew considerable media and public attention, and when he was subpoenaed for the trial, he . . . well, something happened. Depending on who you ask, Clinton either died of scarlet fever pretty much on the spot, committed suicide or used his connections – he was, among other things, the godson of then prime minister William Gladstone – to flee the country and disappear.

We will never know what really became of Lord Arthur, but even if he did die at the age of twenty-nine, his had been a life well lived.

3

The Adventurous

Nothing could prevent Balfour being Prime Minister or MacDonald being Prime Minister, but Cunninghame Graham achieved the adventure of being Cunninghame Graham.

G. K. Chesterton on, well,
Cunninghame Graham

Cunninghame Graham (1852–1936)

MP for North-West Lanarkshire, 1886–92

Most MPs featured in this book have one thing in common: whatever they did to merit the title of honourable misfit either happened in Parliament or out of it. If they were a remarkable (or remarkably bad) politician, chances are there won't be much to say about their time before or after the Commons; if they did or said some incredible or terrible things away from Westminster, chances are their career on the green benches was only a footnote in their life.

Cunninghame Graham is an exception, and was one of a kind both in Parliament and out of it. Brought up between Renfrewshire and Dunbartonshire by a Scottish father and a half-Spanish mother, his first language was Spanish. After going to school in Harrow, he finished his education in Brussels, then moved to Argentina at seventeen to be on his family's cattle ranch.

Between there, Paraguay and Uruguay he built himself a fortune as a gaucho and became renowned enough to gain the affectionate nickname Don Roberto. After meeting the woman who would become his wife – painter, poet and botanist Gabriela de la Balmondière – the pair travelled up to Mexico City, where he taught fencing for a while, then up to Texas, where, among other things, he became friends with Buffalo Bill.

The adventures (temporarily) came to an end in 1883 when his father died and he returned to Britain with a new-found interest in politics. Naturally leaning to the left despite his aristocratic background, Graham found himself meeting Keir Hardie, William Morris and others, and soon joined the socialist cause.

He stood for election in 1886 as a Liberal candidate, but on a platform of Scottish Home Rule, abolition of the House of Lords, universal suffrage and an eight-hour work day, and won fairly comfortably. Once in the Commons, he quickly made himself known by repeatedly getting suspended, including once for saying the word 'damn' in the Chamber, making him the first ever MP to get suspended for swearing.

A prominent advocate of free speech and civil liberties, he took part in the Trafalgar Square protest later known as Bloody Sunday, where he was beaten by the police, arrested, charged and subsequently convicted to six weeks in Pentonville Prison.

His incarceration didn't dampen his spirits one bit. Less than a year later he was suspended from the Commons again, this time for arguing for better working conditions for chain makers and, when reprimanded by the Speaker, shooting back 'I never withdraw',* a line which was stolen by George Bernard Shaw for his play *Arms and the Man*.

Always on the side of the workers, he was involved in the

---

* Quiet at the back.

1889 Dockers' Strike, went to Paris that same summer to attend the Marxist Congress of the Second International, and was arrested in Calais and then sent back to Britain a year later for giving a speech deemed too revolutionary.

Another topic close to his heart was Scottish independence; he was one of the co-founders of the Scottish Home Rule Association, which in 1888 called for 'the establishment of a Scotch national Parliament and an Executive Government having control over exclusively Scotch affairs'. In that same year he also co-founded the Scottish Labour Party with Hardie, though only formally leaving the Liberals in 1892 to stand for election as a Labour candidate.

He lost his seat as a result, but did not lay idle. In 1894 he tried and failed to prospect for gold in Spain, then started writing sketches – mostly of South America and Scotland – for the *Saturday Review* a year later.

In 1897 Graham went to Morocco, where he aimed to get to the 'forbidden city' of Taroudant through the Atlas Mountains, where it was said that no Christian had ever been. He tried to disguise himself as a sheikh from Fez and a Turkish doctor, but all his attempts failed; instead, he was captured on the way by the Kaid of Kintafi, who ruled the area.

He was kept prisoner in a medieval castle for four months but, once released, turned his ordeal into a book: *Mogreb-el-Acksa: A Journey in Morocco*. His most famous literary friendship was with Joseph Conrad, whom he introduced to his publisher, and for years afterwards a portrait of Graham appeared on the cover of the Penguin editions of Conrad's *Nostromo*.

His travelling years didn't end there, as records of letters he sent to his mother show that he was in Uruguay in 1914–15 buying remount horses for the British Army, and in Colombia in 1917 investigating beef cattle resources.

Still, this did not entirely distract him from his political endeavours, as in 1928 he helped launch the National Party of Scotland and was elected honorary president of the newly founded Scottish National Party in 1934.

Though he was in his eighties by that point, Graham was still very active, continuing to write, ride daily and retain some involvement in Scottish politics. In fact, he died of pneumonia in 1936 while in Buenos Aires, where he had returned to visit the birthplace of his friend, fellow author William Hudson.

He was laid in state in the capital city and received a tribute from the president, and a street was later named after him in Buenos Aires. His body was eventually shipped home to Scotland, and brought to the island of Inchmahome in the Trossachs, on the Lake of Menteith.

It was there, in the abandoned ruins of the Augustinian priory, that he had dug his wife's grave himself after she'd passed in 1906, and that he was laid to rest thirty years later – right next to her.

Katharine Stewart-Murray (1874–1960)

MP for Kinross and West Perthshire, 1923–38

As you may have noticed, few women feature in these pages. While this book does not claim that they are in any way less capable of being odd or living messy lives, it is true that in their early years, female MPs were largely well behaved. Well, most of them.

Katharine Ramsay was a Scottish aristocrat educated in London. Unusually for someone who would later become an MP herself, she was first known as a prominent speaker and campaigner against votes for women in Scotland, and by 1913 was the vice-president of her local Anti-Suffrage League branch.

Still, she also spent those years working in local government and served on the Highlands and Islands Medical Service Committee, which played a part in the eventual founding of the NHS some years later.

While her husband went to fight in the Dardanelles campaign during the First World War, she volunteered to work in field hospitals, and received a damehood for her efforts. The Duchess of Atholl, as she was then known, clearly had complex views on women and politics, as she then stood for election in Kinross and West Perthshire in 1923.

As a Scottish Unionist MP (and the first female MP to represent a Scottish seat), she quickly rose through the ranks, becoming parliamentary secretary to the Board of Education in 1924. She also made herself known – and not always liked – as a tireless campaigner for many international issues, including female genital mutilation in the British colonies.

In 1931 she wrote *The Conscription of a People*, a pamphlet hitting out against the abuses of the Soviet Union. In 1935 she coordinated a full English translation of *Mein Kampf* and distributed it among her fellow MPs to warn them of what was coming. In that same year she (temporarily) resigned the Conservative whip over, among other things, the 'national-socialist tendency' of the party's domestic policies. A friend of Winston Churchill's, she opposed Chamberlain's pro-appeasement policies, and resigned the whip again in 1938, which led to her local party deselecting her. Though she tried standing again as an independent in the by-election – with, somewhat absurdly, the support of both Stalin and Churchill – this was the end of her parliamentary career.

Not that it really mattered; by the late 1930s the duchess had firmly set her sights on more important matters. Elected chair of the National Joint Committee for Spanish Relief in 1937, she led a fact-finding delegation to the Franco dictatorship that year.

Then Foreign Secretary Anthony Eden had backed the trip but only as long as it stayed out of Madrid, as it was too dangerous a place to be. Stewart-Murray had agreed and promised not to visit the capital, then set off for Spain and headed straight for the city.

In fairness, Eden had probably had a point. While the duchess and her delegation were having lunch – in the midst of a city being shelled by Franco – a bomb went off nearby, and she had to be kept back for a bit while human remains were cleaned off her car.

Once back in Britain, she broadcast an appeal for the children of Madrid on BBC radio and published a book on what she had witnessed – *Searchlight on Spain* – which became a bestseller. The Red Duchess was born. With the help of Labour politician Leah Manning, she launched and fundraised for the Committee for the Basque Children, which brought nearly four thousand kids to safety in Britain, including forty – and some of their mothers – who came to live in her castle.

Though Spain was her main focus, Stewart-Murray also spent the last few years before the Second World War leading a delegation to Yugoslavia, Romania and Czechoslovakia, going on a speaking tour of Austria for the International Peace Campaign and trying, in vain, to warn Chamberlain against the dangers of Hitler.

As the war raged on, she became honorary colonel of the Regiment of Scottish Horse, and, in 1944, broadcast a message of support to Polish people fighting the Nazis in Warsaw. A few years later she would publish *The Tragedy of Warsaw and Its Documentation* at the request of the Polish government in exile.

This was part of a wider pattern. Once the war was over, the Red Duchess turned her attention to the Soviet Union once more, focusing on the Communists' treatment of people in Hungary and Czechoslovakia and chairing the British League for European Freedom until her death.

Or, as her friend Mary Stocks once put it: 'the Duchess opposed cruelty with a consistency which bred indifference to the political colours of its perpetrators'.

Sitwell Sitwell (1769–1811)

MP for West Looe, 1796–1802

How much can you love a name? If you're Francis Hurt, the answer is: a lot. In 1776, Hurt inherited the wealth and estate of his mother's cousin, whose last name was Sitwell, and decided to change his name to Francis Sitwell in celebration.

There was one small issue with this, namely that he had a seven-year-old son whose first name was Sitwell; thus, Sitwell Sitwell was born. As a young man, Sitwell – or, to use his full name, Sitwell Sitwell – fell in love with the daughter of a merchant whom his father thought wasn't good enough for the Sitwell family.*

Young Sitwell was sent off on a grand tour of Europe, as was common for men of his age and class, and while in Constantinople he was informed that his beloved Alice Parke had died. We can only assume that Sitwell's plan had been for Sitwell to dry his tears on the Continent, then move on; but instead Sitwell rushed back to England to find Parke alive, and was finally allowed to marry her.

In late 1795 he decided he fancied standing for Parliament, so asked the Duke of Portland for a seat and was given one. According to parliamentary records, he never made a speech in the Chamber, and decided to stand down in 1802. To be fair, he was clearly busy elsewhere; when a Bengal tiger escaped from a circus menagerie in Sheffield in 1798, he hunted and killed it.

Still, Sitwell Sitwell's main achievement, at least from the Sitwell family perspective, was to build a grand new ballroom at Renishaw Hall and organise a lavish ball for the Prince of Wales in 1808, bagging a baronetcy in the process. In fact, there is still a Sitwell baronet alive today, though it must tragically be noted that his first name is not Sitwell.

---

* You could even say that the prospect of this engagement did not . . . sit well with him.

Tom Driberg (1905–76)

MP for Maldon, 1942–55

MP for Barking, 1959–74

Tom Driberg had, Christopher Hitchens wrote after his death, 'been indubitably the most consecrated blowjob artist ever to take his seat in either House'. That he found a passion and managed to elevate it to an art should be an inspiration to us all, but his sexual appetite is only one of the many things he should be remembered for. Let's start at the beginning . . .

Born in Sussex, Tom Driberg attended the Grange school in Crowborough, where he messed around with other boys and discovered High Anglicanism. Equally formative were his years at Lancing College near Worthing, where he was bullied but eventually befriended Evelyn Waugh and started writing poetry.

At around fifteen he joined the British Communist Party but still became the deputy head boy, chief sacrist and head librarian of the school. Sadly, he lost all three titles when he was found to have made advances towards two of his classmates, but was kept on out of compassion for his recently widowed mother. Despite being moved away from the other boys for the rest of his time at the school, he did manage to get a scholarship to study classics at Oxford.

A contemporary of W. H. Auden, Harold Acton and many others, Driberg grew fond (or even fonder) of partying, literature and the arts, later explaining that 'there was just no time for any academic work'. Still, he wrote some verse and came to the attention of Edith Sitwell, who declared him 'the hope of English poetry'.

He also got arrested during the General Strike of 1926 and stood for the presidency of the Oxford Union, coming a very reasonable second. Another amusing footnote is the 'concert' he organised called 'Homage to Beethoven', which involved typewriters, megaphones and a flushing toilet. The hoax grabbed the attention of the press, then of Aleister Crowley, and the student and the occultist became acquaintances. Though Crowley wanted Driberg to eventually replace him as 'world teacher' – what an offer! – nothing came of it. Still, young Tom was given several books and manuscripts, which he later sold for good money.

As an entirely unsurprising result of all the above, Tom Driberg left Oxford University in 1927 with no degree. Not that it really mattered; though he spent some time pennilessly living in London, he did so while attending parties at Edith Sitwell's house. Taken by her youthful friend's lack of funds, she got him an interview at the *Daily Express*, who gave him a six-week trial in January 1928.

Perhaps unexpectedly for someone so left wing, Driberg quickly found his feet as a society columnist, getting gossip-filled scoops about parties attended by posh socialites. This led him to a full-time job at the paper on 'The Talk of London', first as an assistant and then as editor of the column.*

In 'The Talk of London' he announced Evelyn Waugh's conversion to Roman Catholicism – to which he had been

---

* He said at the time that his work as a diarist was satirical and aimed to expose the grotesque lifestyles of the rich to the working class in the hope that they might rise up. As a former diarist herself, the author is guessing that, instead, it may just have been a very fun job.

the only witness – and frequently broke stories (and tittle-tattle) about 'men and women who matter', under the byline William Hickey. Though we'll never know if he really was a communist with fiendish intentions or just a young hack keen on sipping champagne with shiny people, Driberg will always be the man who created the gossip column as we know it today.

He also certainly benefited from the status the job gave him in the *Express* newsroom. As is often tradition with diarists, Driberg eventually became close to Lord Beaverbrook, the owner of the paper, who realised his star columnist was frequently out of pocket and offered him loans and gifts.

Money wasn't his only problem, however. After discovering his fondness for sex with men as a teenager, Driberg developed a pronounced taste for casual encounters – not always in the most private of places, and at a time when homosexuality was still illegal. He generally managed to get away with it; when done for indecent assault for a night in bed with two Scottish men, Beaverbrook hired him an expensive barrister and found him some impeccable character witnesses. Once the case was won, he also managed to keep everything out of the press.

After some travelling to Spain, Germany, Italy and the United States on reporting trips, Driberg got stuck back in England when the Second World War broke out in 1939. He used the time to buy Bradwell Lodge, a country house in Essex, with money he'd inherited from his mother earlier that year. In 1941 he was kicked out of the Communist Party, though we're still not sure why. According to some sources, it was because of his lack of support for the Nazi–Soviet

Pact; according to others, he was suspected of having passed on information to MI5.

In any case, things turned out fine for him – again – as he decided to stand for Parliament in 1942 for the seat of Maldon, taking a three-week holiday from Hickey to do so. Though Beaverbrook and Driberg were still close, the *Express* ran a column making it clear that the paper did not support him as a candidate (which, to be fair, is one way of trying to keep your columnist). Sadly for them it did not work, as Driberg won fair and square, and entered the House of Commons as an independent MP.

He made waves straight away, as he used his maiden speech to argue for the ban on the Communist Party's newspaper to be lifted. As he put it, 'one valuable weapon of home propaganda still remains unused, although it would cost the Ministry of Information nothing to use it. I refer to the "Daily Worker".' The plea fell on deaf ears, the chair cutting him off to warn that the point wasn't 'within the scope of the debate'.

Despite becoming a reasonably active MP in the Commons, he still didn't give up on his main pastime, though still retained his ability to get away with just about anything. After getting caught showing a Norwegian sailor a good time in Edinburgh in 1943, he explained to the police officer that he was William Hickey and an MP, and was able to run off into the night.

It is lucky for him that he used the excuse while he still could, as by the end of that year he had been sacked from the *Express* for a story about a minister. He kept writing for the *New Statesman* and other publications and even bagged a regular slot on the BBC European Service, but was soon banned after government pressure.

That clearly didn't bother him too much, as he soon covered the aftermath of D-Day as a war correspondent for left-wing magazine *Reynolds's News* and was part of a delegation of MPs visiting the Buchenwald concentration camp after its liberation in 1945. As the war ended, Driberg jumped ship to the Labour Party, and won his seat again that year in the landslide that made Attlee prime minister.

Not that he seemed overly interested in parliamentary politics by that point. Just days after the election he travelled to Burma to do some more reporting, having managed to become a temporary special adviser to Lord Mountbatten. The highlight of the trip may well have been his visit to nearby Saigon, where he insisted his offer to negotiate with Ho Chi Minh, had it been taken up, would have prevented the Vietnam War altogether.

That he was at most a part-time politician didn't seem to overly bother the Labour Party. In 1949, Driberg was elected onto the National Executive Committee, a spot he kept a year later by being re-elected in absentia while he was away reporting from South Korea. In fact, his main focus wasn't on the Commons even when he was in Britain.

In 1951 he surprised everyone by getting married to a woman, of all people; far from having had a sexual change of heart, it is now largely believed that he needed someone to take care of Bradwell Lodge. The reaction from his peers was mixed – and often downright mean – as his fiancée was not deemed to be very attractive. A memorable example comes from Winston Churchill himself, who is said to have seen a picture of her and quipped that 'buggers can't be choosers'. Charming fellow.

Still, Ena Binfield walked down the aisle to a choral

arrangement of the socialist song 'The Red Flag', and several hundred people partied in the House of Commons afterwards. That it wasn't a very happy marriage shouldn't be a surprise, and that Driberg immediately moved on to other concerns shouldn't be either.

Having retained his seat that same year – albeit with a slimmed down majority – Driberg continued to not take his parliamentary career entirely seriously. In 1953, for example, he showed American singer Johnnie Ray round the Palace, and tried (unsuccessfully) to use the opportunity to get into the celebrity's pants. He announced that he would be standing down a year later but was, as ever, already busy elsewhere.

Driberg was writing a biography of his old acquaintance Beaverbrook; and though the project sounded interesting in theory, in practice the pair of them managed to make the whole thing largely useless. Though Beaverbrook had promised not to intervene editorially, he found the draft of the tome to be showing his author's 'malice and hatred', and insisted on extensive edits. Driberg caved, and the published book was watered down enough to be of little interest, although Beaverbrook used the *Daily Express* to campaign against it anyway. All in all, the story gives credence to the famous Waugh quote: '[O]f course I believe in the devil. How else could I account for Lord Beaverbrook?'

His other non-fiction writing venture was also unconvincing. In 1956 he flew to Moscow to interview Guy Burgess, a British diplomat who had defected to Russia and who he had met in the 1940s. The book that came from the interview only fuelled whispers about Driberg being a spy, though pleasingly the conspiracy went both ways. His portrayal of Burgess had been quite sympathetic, so rumours swirled that the book had been vetted by the KGB and also that it was an MI5 plot to get the former diplomat to reveal as much as possible so that he could be charged if he ever set foot in Britain again. No proof from either side ever surfaced, so we can probably conclude it was just a not very good book, written by someone in urgent need of money.

Luckily this was the end of his foray into publishing, at least for a while. After doing some more travelling – including several meetings with Nikita Khrushchev – Driberg decided to stand for Parliament again in 1959, and became the MP for Barking. He was a more active backbencher this time around, although it didn't necessarily help the Labour leadership, or his constituency. Instead, he focused on nuclear disarmament and other issues personally close to his heart, and in 1964 he joined the Tribune group of MPs, intending to drag Harold Wilson more to the left.

This doesn't mean he wasn't also keeping busy on the side. A year earlier, he had made the acquaintance of the Kray twins, the East London club owners and all-round criminals. Along with Conservative peer Lord Boothby, Driberg attended parties at the twins' flat, where young working-class men from the East End were provided as entertainment. Unsurprisingly, the press caught wind of it quickly enough, and the *Sunday Mirror* published an exposé on Boothby's sexual relationship with Ronnie Kray, which was still a crime at the time.

Worried that any further investigations would involve Tom Driberg and damage the Labour Party, Wilson offered his solicitor to Boothby. Happily for the pair of them (but sadly for press freedom), the *Sunday Mirror* eventually retracted its story, apologised formally to Boothby, paid him £40,000 in an out-of-court settlement, and sacked its editor. Since other papers didn't want to risk the same fate, the story was dropped altogether and – once again – Driberg got away with it.

In fact he moved on pretty quickly, and by 1965 was busy spending time around Mick Jagger, trying to convince him to stand as a Labour candidate. Staying true to himself, he is also said to have remarked 'Oh my, Mick, what a big basket you have!' Despite still sending on bits of gossip to *Private Eye* and occasionally writing their cryptic crossword, Driberg now found his journalism work largely drying up.

Though he had wanted to stand down in 1970, he remained in the Commons in order to keep his salary before finally leaving in 1974. He wrote another biography – this time of Hannen Swaffer, a journalist – which once again received a lukewarm reception and was swiftly forgotten. Still, things picked up again briefly in 1975, when his friends threw him a lavish seventieth birthday party – attended, as he remarked on the day, by 'one duke, two dukes' daughters, sundry lords, a bishop, a poet laureate' – and later that year he was granted a life peerage.

While attending the Lords in 1976, he was also writing his memoirs, but sadly did not get to finish them; on 12 August he had a heart attack while riding in a cab, which turned out to be fatal. The unfinished *Ruling Passions*, an honest account of his career as well as his sexual encounters, was published a year later. He had picked the title himself; according to Hitchens, 'the pun was at his expense, since he did precious little ruling and his passions did the rest'. Oh, and we never did find out if he really was a spy. What a life, eh?

Edward Wortley Montagu (1713–76)

MP for Bossiney, 1747

MP for Huntingdonshire, 1747–54

MP for Bossiney, 1754–68

Some people just cannot sit still. The son of an MP and a traveller, it should not be a surprise that Edward Wortley Montagu was mostly interested in travelling and politics; still, he pushed things to a level even his parents resented.

As a toddler, he was brought to Constantinople and Pera, a district of Istanbul in Turkey, where he became the first British-born person to get inoculated for smallpox. Once back in England he was placed at the prestigious Westminster School, but would not stop escaping. There was the time he ran away and was eventually found in Oxford; the time he was found, after a year, selling fish in east London. Then there was the time he managed to make his way to Portugal, where he worked in vineyards and took care of donkeys until he was arrested and brought back to his parents.

Since he was clearly keen on spending time abroad anyway, Montagu was then sent to the West Indies with a tutor, and to Leiden University in the Netherlands, where he learnt Arabic. He joined the army in 1743, rising to the rank of captain lieutenant in the 1st Regiment of Foot, fought in the War of the Austrian Succession, and became an MP in 1747.

Despite attending the conference that ended the war in Aix-la-Chapelle and generally being liked by Lord Sandwich, whom he worked for, Montagu was despised by his parents.

His father had, by that point, broken the entail on the family's estates in order to eventually disinherit him, and forbidden him from sitting close to him in the chamber of the House of Commons. Though he was giving him an allowance of £1,000 a year, it was under the condition that the two were never in the same city, forcing the son to leave Paris in November 1750 as his father was arriving.

Montagu was a well-known character back in England, prompting the writer Horace Walpole to remark:

> His father scarce allows him anything: yet he plays, dresses, diamonds himself, even to distinct shoe-buckles for a frock, and has more snuff boxes than would suffice a Chinese idol with an hundred noses. But the most curious part of his dress, which he has brought from Paris, is an iron wig; you literally would not know it from hair.

In 1751, he and a fellow MP of dubious morals Theobald Taaffe set up in London as faro bankers for the French ambassador, then moved to Paris later that year. Once there, the pair were arrested for cheating a Jewish man at cards, then burgling his house when he didn't pay up. Montagu spent eleven days in a French prison, but in the end got away with only a fine.

He returned to England and resumed his (largely idle) parliamentary career after his father, in an uncharacteristic show of paternal care, got him the seat of Bossiney in 1754 to keep his creditors at bay.

In 1759 he published *Reflections on the Rise and Fall of the Ancient Republicks*, a book on the Seven Years' War, which had been raging since 1756, and looked to the ancient republics of Rome, Athens, Thebes, Sparta and Carthage for answers to Britain's plight.

After standing down, he spent his remaining years in the Mediterranean, where he designed and published detailed maps of northern Greece. By that point he spoke fluent Arabic, Dutch, Hebrew and Persian, among other languages, and died in his early sixties in Venice. His parents thought him mad until the very end; when his mother passed away, she left him a single guinea in her will.

Brook Watson (1735–1807)

MP for London, 1784–93

Born in Plymouth, Brook Watson became an orphan in 1741 and was sent to live with relatives in Boston, Massachusetts. At fourteen he became a crew member on one of his uncle's merchant ships and travelled to Havana, Cuba, where disaster struck. Watson was out swimming in the harbour when he was attacked by a shark; with its first bite it stripped the flesh of his right leg up to the calf; with the second, the right foot was off. He was rescued by his shipmates but the limb had to be amputated, and he spent the rest of his life with a wooden right leg.

That did not stop him from working with the British Army as a commissary – earning the irritatingly unoriginal moniker of wooden-legged commissary – and being a successful merchant. While sailing around the world on business, Watson made the acquaintance of John Singleton Copley, and commissioned him to paint *Watson and the Shark*, which, again, feels pretty self-explanatory.

The painting was exhibited at the National Gallery in 1778, where it drew considerable attention, and soon after Watson became an alderman of the City of London, then an MP. According to contemporary accounts, his missing limb never caused him any trouble in the Commons, but his personality did. As one poem put it:

> *'One moment's time I presume to beg?'*
> *Cries modest Watson, on his wooden leg;*
> *That leg, in which such wond'rous art is shewn,*
> *It almost seems to serve him like his own;*
> *Oh! Had the monster, who for breakfast ate*
> *That luckless limb, his nobler noddle met,*
> *The best of workmen, nor the best of wood,*
> *Had scarce supply'd him with Title so good.*

Still, he eventually left Parliament and became Lord Mayor of London and a director of the Bank of England in his later years, so it's fair to say he had the last laugh.

Robert FitzRoy (1805–65)

MP for the City of Durham, 1841–3

A descendant of Charles II, Robert FitzRoy was born into an aristocratic Suffolk family. At the age of twelve he entered the Royal Naval College in Portsmouth, then the Royal Navy a year later. He thereupon embarked aboard the frigate

HMS *Owen Glendower* as a voluntary student in 1820, and got promoted to midshipman before the ship returned from its trip to South America in 1822. By 1824 he had been promoted to lieutenant, after having passed his examination with full marks – the first ever student to do so. Four years later he boarded the HMS *Ganges* as flag lieutenant to Rear Admiral Sir Robert Waller Otway, and headed back to South America. While this journey was underway, Captain Pringle Stokes was working on a hydrographic survey of Tierra del Fuego, an archipelago off the southern tip of Chile and Argentina.

Depressed after spending six months on solitary survey work, he shot himself. The HMS *Beagle* had to be brought back to Rio de Janeiro by a lieutenant, at which point FitzRoy was made temporary captain of the ship. While he and his crew were studying the area, a group of native Fuegians managed to steal one of their boats; in response, FitzRoy captured four young Fuegians and held them as hostages. Eventually, *Beagle* started making its way back to England, with all four natives still on board. For some reason that presumably made more sense at the time, he had decided to teach them English and eventually send them back to their archipelago as Protestant missionaries. One of them tragically died en route after a smallpox vaccination, but the other three, el'leparu, o'run-del'lico and yok'cushly – puzzlingly renamed York Minster, Jemmy Button and Fuegia Basket by the crew – arrived in Plymouth with FitzRoy.

After some months in London, including an audience with King William IV, the three Fuegians and Robert FitzRoy returned to HMS *Beagle*, on their way back to South America. Though the latter's time back home lasted for less than a year, the stay had been eventful. First, he had run for Parliament in Ipswich as a Tory candidate, but been defeated. Then there was the new travel companion he had asked for, wary as he was after having witnessed several captains go mad from isolation and eventually kill themselves.

A few men had been approached but had turned down the opportunity until the appearance of a certain 'Mr Darwin, grandson of the well-known philosopher and poet – full of zeal and enterprize [sic]'. Charles was still but a young naturalist at this point, and was pleased to be going off on an adventure across the world with FitzRoy, whom he called 'everything that is delightful'. The pair got along well at the start of the trip, but spending several years in close quarters with one other person is no easy feat, especially as, towards the end, the captain suffered from 'morbid depression of spirits, & a loss of all decision & resolution'. The two men would also often argue, most famously about the issue of slavery, Darwin having been horrified by the treatment of slaves in Brazil while FitzRoy had been nonplussed at best.

Still, the trip was an overall success, despite Jemmy Button (frankly unsurprisingly) refusing to go back to England and preferring to stay home instead.

After returning in October 1836, FitzRoy set out to marry his long-term fiancée Mary Henrietta O'Brien, sweetly telling Darwin in a letter: 'I am going to be married!!!!!!!' He was awarded a gold medal by the Royal Geographical Society a year later, and set out to write a series of books about his voyage. The four-volume *Narrative of the Surveying Voyages of H.M.S. Adventure and Beagle* was published in 1839, and was overall well received, though not acclaimed enough that he was sent back to sea. Despite being a man of science, he was first and foremost deeply religious, and wrote about much of his surveys through a biblical lens, which may have gained him widespread popularity at some point, but was already somewhat *passé* by then.

Instead, he returned to his other interest: politics. In 1841 he was elected as the Tory MP for Durham, but staying both still and in England was never going to suit him entirely. A mere two years later the government found itself in need of a new governor of New Zealand, and FitzRoy fitted the bill perfectly. He resigned from the Commons in 1843 and set out on yet another journey across the world.

Sadly, his governorship did not turn out to be a successful one. Most of the job entailed managing the increasingly fraught relationship between the native Maori and the settlers and missionaries pouring into the country, which he failed at. In fact, the Flagstaff War, which raged for ten months between the British and Maori tribes, exploded under his watch. In fairness to him, the job he had been given was a near impossible one to accomplish with no funds, and his multiple requests for financial support had been denied by the government. He was eventually recalled and came back to Britain in 1848.

After a couple of years back on a ship, he left the Navy, was elected to the Royal Society and started working on his final act. In 1854, FitzRoy was appointed as the head of a newly created department at the Board of Trade, aiming to collect weather data at sea. Thanks to him, information about upcoming weather events was widely distributed to fishermen, and he oversaw the installation of barometers at every port, so sailors could check the conditions before heading to their ships. Following a storm that caused the wreck of a large steam clipper in 1859, he started making charts predicting future weather, which he dubbed 'weather forecasts'.

In 1860 he had storm warning cones installed in major ports and hoisted when there was a risk of gales, and in 1861 *The Times* started publishing a daily weather forecast, all thanks to him. By then, FitzRoy's work was so trusted that Queen Victoria had him draw up a forecast for a journey she was about to make to her home on the Isle of Wight. Tragically, his depression caught up with him eventually, and in 1865 he cut his throat with a razor. When given the news, his old friend Charles Darwin was surprised at first, but added: 'I ought not to have been, for I remember once thinking it likely.'

He was buried in All Saints' Church in Upper Norwood, in a grave that was later restored by the Meteorological Office in 1981.

James Patrick Mahon (1800?–91)

MP for County Clare, 1830

MP for Ennis, 1847–52

MP for County Clare, 1879–85

James Patrick Mahon was a character. We cannot say for sure what he was or wasn't up to since, as his parliamentary biography dryly puts it, 'The O'Gorman Mahon, a grotesque character even by the exotic standards of some of the Irish Members in this period, was a figure of pure self-invention.' Still, we will have to take his word for some of what follows, even if some of it sounds somewhat extravagant.

James Patrick Mahon was born at some point between 1799 and 1803, perhaps in March, perhaps not. His family were prominent Roman Catholics in County Clare, and he went to boarding school, then to Trinity College, Dublin, where he got a degree and a masters in law. When his father died in 1821, he inherited half the family's property, and around then he decided to call himself 'the O'Gorman Mahon'. O'Gorman was his mother's maiden name, but the new moniker was meant to make him sound like the head of the Mahon clan.

He married a rich heiress in 1830 and joined the Catholic Association, which got him into politics. That year, he was elected as the MP for County Clare, and was a popular figure in his area. As fellow Irish politician Richard Sheil wrote around then:

He has a very striking physiognomy, of the corsair character . . . His figure is tall and he is peculiarly free and *dégagé* in all his attitudes and movements. In any other his attire would appear singularly fantastical. His manners are exceedingly frank and natural, and have a character of kindliness as well as of self-reliance imprinted upon them . . . When O'Gorman Mahon throws himself out before the people, and, touching his whiskers with one hand, brandishes the other, an enthusiasm is at once produced, to which the fair portion of the spectators lend their tender contribution.

His beginnings in the Commons were not quite so successful. As MP William Nugent Macnamara wrote to his brother in November: 'O'G. M. is here. He told me he would support ministers though he came shortly after and sat next [to] me on the opposition bench. In fact, he is insincere and deceitful. He does not seem to know anyone here.' Then there was the time he missed a crucial division because he was busy having dinner. In any case, he was quickly unseated following allegations of bribery, and despite being acquitted afterwards, he failed to regain his seat in the election of 1831.

This wasn't a problem for Mahon, though, as he knew how to keep himself busy. After leaving politics, he became deputy lieutenant of Clare and captain of the local militia, then decided to do some travelling. In 1835 he went to Paris, where he became a journalist, friend of the Prince of Talley-rand and a favourite at the court of Louis-Philippe. After that came a trip to Africa where, among other things, he made the acquaintance of Ferdinand de Lesseps, who would later work on the Suez Canal.

He returned to Ireland in 1846 and got elected as the MP for Ennis a year later, this time as a Whig and supporter of the Repeal Association, which campaigned to end the Acts of Union of 1800 between Ireland and Great Britain. After losing his seat again in 1852, he decided to resume his adventures. This is where things get a bit tricky – we know the O'Gorman Mahon liked telling stories about himself, and we know that there is not a whole lot of evidence that he did everything he said he did. If we are to take him at his word, however, we would find that he did get up to a lot in those years.

First, he went back to Paris, but soon afterwards he travelled to St Petersburg, where he ended up becoming lieutenant in the Imperial Bodyguard of the tsar and once went bear-hunting with the tsar's son across Finland and Siberia. After that, he journeyed across China and India and served in the Austrian and Ottoman armies as a mercenary, before popping back to England in 1858. A year later he was in South America, attempting to get funds for the construction of a canal through Central America and investigating the disappearance of a British commander, pushing the Peruvian government into their own investigation, which found that he had been murdered.

Clearly at home in armies, he then joined the Uruguayan Civil War as a general in the government forces and the Chincha Islands War as commander of a Chilean fleet. He also allegedly joined the Brazilian army as a colonel under Emperor Dom Pedro II, and was made a bishop while in the country. When the American Civil War broke out he decided that he simply had to get involved, and travelled to fight for the Union. Once he was done with the Americas, he returned to France where he became a colonel in a regiment of chasseurs under Louis-Napoleon. Finally, the last stop on his world tour was Germany, where he became close to future chancellor Otto von Bismarck.

Having entirely run out of money by that point, Mahon returned to Ireland, and in 1879 was back in the House of Commons as the MP for County Clare. There, he worked closely with famous Irish nationalist politician Charles Stewart Parnell, having himself stood on a platform of Home Rule. By that point, the O'Gorman Mahon was more liked than he had been when he first represented the constituency over fifty years previously. In 1889, William Ewart Gladstone wrote that the 'Commons is now familiar with the stately figure of an Irish gentleman advanced in life, who carries with him the halo of an extraordinary reputation in that particular, but who is conspicuous among all his contemporaries for his singularly beautiful and gentle manners'.

This was, allegedly, a wink to his duelling habit, as Mahon liked to claim that he'd instigated and fought thirteen duels (and won a majority of them, of course). As with everything else, there is almost certainly some truth to this, but we will never know how much. What we do know is that he won his last election in 1887 at (probably) eighty-seven, making him the oldest MP in Parliament at that point, and that he died four years later, while still serving.

Oliver Baldwin (1899–1958)

MP for Dudley, 1929–31

MP for Paisley, 1945–7

When Oliver Baldwin was born in 1899, his father Stanley, one day to become prime minister of Great Britain, was a mere businessman. Still, he was a wealthy enough one to send his son to Eton, though with mixed results. According to his *Who's Who* entry, he was educated 'in football at Eton; in other things, beginning to learn', and his teachers found him to be 'full of silliness, egotism, un-divine discontent, contempt for others [and of course for authority, discipline, tradition, etc.]'.

What he really wanted was to go to war, which he was finally allowed to do in 1917 when he was commissioned in the Irish Guards, then in 1918 when he got to fight in France in the First World War. Then, after a brief spell as British vice consul in Boulogne, he went travelling across North Africa. Unusually for a young man from a moneyed family, he refused to be financially supported by his father, choosing instead to make a living as a journalist and travel writer.

Still, his fondness for the army never went away, and by 1920 he (somehow) found himself an infantry instructor in the newly independent republic of Armenia. The timing was unfortunate, as the democratic government fell apart soon afterwards, resulting in him getting thrown into jail by Bolshevik-backed revolutionaries. Though he was released two months later when democracy was restored, this was not the end of his troubles. On his way back to Britain, Baldwin was arrested by Turkish authorities who, clearly stung by his support for Armenia, decided he was a Soviet spy. He was imprisoned for seven months in bleak conditions, but did finally manage to get back to England after that.

Once back home he got engaged to Dorothea Arbuthnot, but the pair never married as Arbuthnot unfortunately was of the wrong gender. Instead, Baldwin started a relationship with Johnnie Boyle and went to live in Oxfordshire. Their time there sounds idyllic: they raised turkeys, welcomed a wide range of guests, and devotedly referred to each other as 'koot' (from 'queer as a coot'). His biographer Christopher J. Walker described their domestic set-up as 'one of gentle, amicable, animal-loving primitive homosexual socialism', which does sound enticing.

Speaking of socialism – after some years spent hovering around political circles, Baldwin was eventually elected as the Labour MP for Dudley in 1929, which was a tad awkward for all involved as it was the same election his father had lost as leader of the Conservative Party. Still, father and son got along well, and Oliver's sexual orientation had been accepted by his family. After some tumultuous but not very interesting years in and out of Parliament (and a stint in the Second World War that is not especially worthy of mention either), Baldwin inherited his father's earldom and became a peer in 1947.

A year later he was appointed governor of the Leeward Islands, then a British colony in the Caribbean. Boyle in tow, he moved to the island and had a lovely time there, at least according to reports of skinny dipping with visiting sailors and the frequent appearance of steel bands. Still, his sincere belief in not only socialism but multiracial inclusiveness is what eventually led to him getting recalled in 1950 by the British government.

Though he died eight years later, his fondness for the place – or perhaps the time he spent there – was made clear by the fact that his ashes were buried on a hilltop in Antigua, in the Leeward Islands. He may never have achieved a parliamentary career quite like his father's, but Oliver did manage to leave behind a prominent career in anti-fascist journalism, and still had Johnnie Boyle at his side when he passed away.

David James (1919–86)

MP for Brighton Kemptown, 1959–64

MP for North Dorset, 1970–79

The son of a Conservative MP, David James was born in 1919 and educated at – you'll never guess! – Eton. At seventeen he left school and became a trainee officer, sailing around the world in a four-masted steel barque called *Viking*. Continuing his particularly thrilling gap years, he went to Spain with his father to observe the Spanish Civil War before finally ending up – again, a huge surprise – at Balliol College, Oxford. Not one for academia, he left the university less than two years later to join the Royal Navy Reserve, and in June 1940 joined HMS *Drake* as a midshipman.

After working on a number of different ships, he found himself on Motor Gun Boat 79 in February 1943 when it got sunk in action off the coast of the Netherlands. He and three of his men were rescued by a German trawler, then promptly sent off to Marlag O, a naval prisoner-of-war camp. After several months of imprisonment, James decided to try and escape in December that year. On a conveniently foggy morning, he managed to slip out of the shower block and off the ship. Though wearing his British naval uniform, he travelled through Germany under the fake name I. Bagerov, thanks to some forged papers from the Bulgarian navy.

In fact, he made it all the way to Lübeck, in the north of the country, at which point he made contact with the crew of a Swedish ship who agreed to smuggle him out and back to Allied territory. Sadly, he was caught before this could happen, and sent back to Marlag O. A year later he slipped out of the shower block once more and headed towards the Baltic Sea, this time pretending to be a merchant seaman. The second time turned out to be the charm as he did make it to Sweden, then safely returned to Britain.

Back home, he received an OBE, taught fellow members of the Navy escape tactics and wrote a book about his time in Germany called *Escaper's Progress*. He also participated in Operation Tabarin, a secret expedition to the Antarctic seeking to establish British bases in the area as well as collecting meteorological and topographical data and samples of fossils, rocks and flora. This offered James a nice segue into his next act, as he was appointed polar adviser to director Charles Frend in 1948 for his movie *Scott of the Antarctic*. Adept at milking his adventures for all their worth, he ended up being actor John Mills's body double in several scenes, and wrote, not one but two books on his time spent in the Antarctic.

Clearly deciding that writing was something he enjoyed, James then spent a decade publishing books. Among other things, he co-edited a collection of wartime Navy stories and a series of essays entitled *In Praise of Fox Hunting*, and wrote a biography of British military commander Lord Roberts of Kandahar. The end of the 1950s marked the beginning of James's last act: in 1959 he became the Conservative MP for Brighton Kemptown.

His time in the House of Commons was not especially impressive. Some of his ideas were on the quirkier side, as shown by the time when, in 1961, he tried to convince the government to set up prison colonies on the uninhabited islands off the west coast of Scotland. Still, he did gain notoriety a year later by being one of the co-founders of the Loch Ness Phenomena Investigation Bureau. Pretty convinced the monster was real, the outfit aimed to 'study Loch Ness to identify the creature known as the Loch Ness Monster or determine the causes of reports of it'.

How did they do this, you ask? Well, it's easy, really: they encouraged groups of volunteers (self-funded, of course) to watch Loch Ness from different vantage points, using film cameras with telescopic lenses to capture any conclusive or at least intriguing sights. By the end of the 1960s there were

1,030 members, including 588 in Britain. Sadly, the Loch Ness Investigation Bureau (LNIB), as it was later renamed, put a temporary end to James's political career.

In the election of 1964 he lost his seat to the Labour candidate by seven votes, and it was thought at the time that his eccentric obsession with the Loch Ness monster had played a part in his downfall. Still, he did manage to get re-elected six years later, this time as the MP for North Dorset, a position he kept until he retired in 1979. Sadly, the LNIB had been disbanded for several years by that point, and he died without ever getting confirmation that the monster did exist.

4

The Lustful and the Idle

A bounder but not a cad.

The Queen Mother (allegedly)
on Baron Boothby

Harold Nicolson (1886–1968)

MP for Leicester West, 1935–45

Harold Nicolson had a dream of a childhood. The son of a diplomat, he was born in Tehran, then spent his formative years following his father's postings and living between Russia, Turkey, Spain, Bulgaria and Morocco. In 1900 he was back in Britain and attended Wellington College, then moved on to Balliol College, Oxford, four years later. According to his biographer Thomas G. Otte, his university years were well spent: 'after the conventional dullness of Wellington, Nicolson flourished in Balliol's liberal and cerebrally stimulating climate'.

Still, those years probably were a bit too well spent, as he came out of Oxford with a third-class degree. Because he was bright and well heeled, this didn't really matter. In 1909 he joined the diplomatic service after passing its competitive exams, and soon became an attaché in Madrid. In 1910 he met novelist Vita Sackville-West for the first time, and the pair immediately got along. In Vita's (charming) words:

> He was as gay and clever as ever, and I loved his brain and his youth, and was flattered at his liking for me. He

came to Knole a good deal that autumn and winter, and people began to tell me he was in love with me, which I didn't believe was true, but wished that I could believe it. I wasn't in love with him then – there was Rosamund – but I did like him better than anyone, as a companion and playfellow, and for his brain and his delicious disposition.

The one issue, as you may have gleaned, was that Sackville-West was rather busy sleeping with women at the time, and initially turned down Nicolson's proposal in early 1912. She relented after some pressure from her mother, and the couple married the following year, though she had no intention of being faithful to her new husband.

Instead, she continued her relationship with Rosamund Grosvenor, and the one with Violet Keppel, and probably some other ones too. In all fairness, Nicolson was also pursuing some relationships with men on the side, so bisexuality was very much built into the marriage. This does not mean it wasn't a loving union; the pair would write to each other every day when living apart, and they did have several children together.

Meanwhile, Nicolson's diplomatic career was going from strength to strength; he handed Britain's revised declaration of war to the German ambassador in 1914 and was at the Paris Peace Conference in 1918. After a light bout of drama in 1920 when Sackville-West escaped to France with yet another woman, he was appointed private secretary to the Secretary General of the League of Nations. He became a senior diplomat in Tehran in 1925, then in Berlin in 1928, before leaving the diplomatic service altogether in 1929.

By that point he had also gained a reputation as a fairly renowned writer, having published a book on Paul Verlaine in 1921, Alfred Tennyson in 1923, Lord Byron in 1924, and a handful of others. In 1930 he took up a job as editor of the 'Londoner's Diary', the *Evening Standard*'s famous gossip column, which he ended up hating. This is what he wrote in his own diary around a year after joining the newsroom:

> I have found my feet in the *Standard* office – and [newspaper owner] Beaverbrook likes me. But that is all very well. I was not made to be a journalist and I do not want to go on being one. It is a mere expense of spirit in a waste of shame. A constant triviality which is bad for the mind. Goodness knows what I shall do next year. I am on the verge of politics. I stand on the verge of leaving the *Evening Standard* and either writing books of my own or sitting in the House of Commons. 1931 assuredly will be the most important year for good or ill, in my whole life.

Teenage tone aside, he did do exactly what he set out to do; he left the *Standard* in 1931 and joined Oswald Mosley's New Party and stood for election the same year, but failed to gain a seat. It was probably for the best as Mosley formed the British Union of Fascists a year later, which Nicolson wanted nothing to do with. Instead, he was elected in 1935 as a National Labour MP and, in a pleasing turn of events, became one of the first parliamentarians to warn the government about the rise of fascism. (It must be said, however, that his stance on the issue was muddled at best, as he once wrote: 'although I loathe antisemitism [*sic*] I do dislike Jews' – a statement considerably less than ideal.)

An ardent Francophile, he was heartbroken by the country's certain defeat early on in the war, writing in his diary: 'June 12, 1940. I saw [author] André Maurois in the morning. He left Paris yesterday. He said that never before in his life had he experienced such agony as he did when he saw Paris basking under a lovely summer day and realised that he might never see it again. I do feel so deeply for the French.' His love for the country was such that when he was finally able to go back in 1945, he kissed the ground.

Sadly, his love for countries didn't always extend to caring for their people, as he had got in hot water a year previously for arguing against the destruction of the Monte Cassino abbey in Italy, despite it being used to fire at the Allied forces standing below. In *The Spectator*, he had written that the moral choice was to let thousands of men die – including his own son, who was fighting in the area – instead of destroying a great work of art containing many works of art within it. The column went down as well as you would expect, and the abbey was destroyed by American bombers days later.

He lost his seat in 1945, joined the Labour Party in an unsuccessful bid to try and get a peerage, then failed to get re-elected a few years later, putting a firm end to his political career. The last two decades of his life were decidedly calmer. He published a number of other books but did not do much else. Despite all the straying, he and Vita Sackville-West remained together until she died in 1962. He followed her to the grave six years later, and the couple are buried together at their residence, Sissinghurst Castle in Kent.

Robert Boothby (1900–1986)

MP for Aberdeen and Kincardine East, 1924–50

MP for Aberdeenshire Eastern, 1950–8

The son of wealthy Scottish banker Sir Robert Tuite Boothby, Robert Boothby was educated at – all together now! – Eton, then Magdalen College, Oxford. He did relatively little studying there, as, by his own admission, 'there were far too many other things to do'. Instead, he gained the nickname the Palladium, after the central London theatre, as he was 'twice nightly'. After managing a pass without distinction he joined a firm of stockbrokers, but his sights were firmly set on Westminster.

After unsuccessfully standing for the Conservative Party in Orkney and Shetland in 1923, he became the MP for Aberdeen and Kincardine East a year later. His parliamentary career got off to a good start when he was appointed by then chancellor Winston Churchill as his parliamentary private secretary in 1926. Still – and this will become a common refrain – he soon became busy elsewhere.

In 1930 – following the realisation that heterosexual sex could be just as fun as gay dalliances – Boothby started having an affair with Dorothy Macmillan, the wife of fellow MP Harold Macmillan. The next incident worth noting came two years later, when he found himself in Germany and got to meet Adolf Hitler. As he (entertainingly) put it in his memoirs a few decades later:

I received a telephone call from my friend 'Putzi' Hanfstaengl, who was at that time Hitler's personal private secretary and court jester. He told me that the Führer had been reading my speeches with interest, and would like to see me at his headquarters in the Esplanade Hotel.

It is true that when I walked across the long room to a corner in which he was sitting writing, in a brown shirt with a swastika on his arm, he waited without looking up until I had reached his side, then sprang to his feet, lifted his right arm, and shouted 'Hitler!'; and that I responded by clicking my heels together, raising my right arm, and shouting back: 'Boothby!'

On a somewhat more serious note, another thing he took from the meeting was 'the unmistakable glint of madness in his eyes', and he became part of the small group of MPs trying to get the House of Commons to worry about Germany. In fact, this is what he told the Chamber in 1934:

Today Germany is governed by a group of able and ruthless men, who have persuaded the German people that they can never become great again except through armed force. I tell you they are rearming. And I say this – that if we go on as we are today, in a year or eighteen months' time they will be in a position to strike a vital blow at the very heart of the British Empire . . . If we are strong and resolute, and if we pursue a wise and constructive foreign policy, we can still save the world from war. But if we simply drift along, never taking the lead, and exposing the heart of our Empire to an attack which might pulverize it in a few hours, then everything that makes life worth living will be swept away.

As we know now, the warning fell on deaf ears. Two years later Boothby became the co-founder of the Popular Front, a cross-party campaign against appeasement which also had little effect on the government of Neville Chamberlain. When Churchill became prime minister in 1940, he brought Boothby back as parliamentary private secretary to the Ministry of Food. Though he did some decent work getting milk to children and nursing mothers during the war, he had to resign only a year later after a select committee revealed he had failed to declare an interest when asking a question in the Chamber.

Despite having returned to the back benches, he managed to keep himself busy during and after the war, becoming, among other things, one of the original members of the Council of United Europe. He rose to prominence again in the early 1950s, when he decided to start campaigning for the decriminalisation of homosexuality. His opening salvo was a memorandum to Home Secretary David Maxwell-Fyfe in 1953, which read:

By attaching so fearful a stigma to homosexuality as such, you put a very large number of otherwise law-abiding and useful citizens on the other side of the fence which divides the good citizen from the bad. By making them feel that, instead of unfortunates they are social pariahs, you drive them into squalor – perhaps into crime; and produce that very 'underground' which it is so clearly in the public interest to eradicate.

He followed this up in the Chamber in 1954, arguing (not unreasonably) that what adults consensually do to one another in private should be 'a moral issue between them and their maker [and] not a legal issue between them and the state'. Then there was his (blunt but not entirely incorrect) point that trying to cure a man's homosexuality by sending him to prison was about as useful as trying to 'rehabilitate a chronic alcoholic by giving him occupational therapy in a brewery'.

The reaction was mixed. On the one hand Maxwell-Fyfe told Boothby he was 'not going down to history as the man who made sodomy legal', but on the other he did set up the Departmental Committee on Homosexual Offences and Prostitution, which called for the decriminalisation of homosexuality in 1957. Sadly for gay and bisexual men everywhere, it would take nearly another decade for the law to change.

This would soon prove to be an issue for Boothby as well, since he was fond of practising what he preached. In 1963, Boothby started sleeping with criminal Leslie Holt. Though himself a mere cat burglar, Holt was an acquaintance of the Kray twins, and soon introduced his new lover to the gangsters. Things went downhill very quickly after that.

Though Boothby's, erm, close friendship with Ronnie Kray only lasted for a matter of months, he managed to have him over for dinner in the House of Lords in that time, allegedly in exchange for the services of young men from the East End Kray could provide. Then there was the drink at White's, the impossibly fancy members' club in central London, and the debauched sex parties in flats owned by the twins.

This double life was unsurprisingly unsustainable, and led to the *Daily Mirror* publishing a front-page story titled 'Peer and a Gangster: Yard Probe' in the summer of 1964. Though they did not name the pair, the paper said it had evidence of a liaison between a 'prominent peer and a leading thug in the London underworld'.

Boothby was holidaying in France with *Daily Telegraph* editor Colin Cootes when the story broke. Once back in London, he called friend and fellow Kray acquaintance Tom Driberg (remember him?) to ask who the peer was. 'I'm sorry Bob, it's you' was the answer. Many more people soon got the answer to the question as well, the *Mirror* having announced that it had a picture of the peer and criminal together while a German paper threw all caution to the wind by publishing the headline 'Lord Bobby in Trouble'.

As you may remember from our adventures with Driberg, Boothby decided to sue the *Mirror* and was provided with fine legal help by the Labour Party, who were getting worried that one of their own was about to go down with the Boothby ship. In the end the *Mirror* had to sack its editor, the politician got a whopping £40,000, and no other newspaper dared touch the story again.

Though he lived on for another twenty years, there is not much else to say about Lord Boothby, who had presumably grown tired of the limelight by that point – and frankly, who could blame him.

William John Bankes (1786–1855)

MP for Truro, 1810–12

MP for Cambridge University, 1822–6

MP for Marlborough, 1829–32

MP for Dorset, 1832–5

The son of an MP on one side and grandson of another on the other, William John Bankes had a lovely time growing up. He studied at Westminster School, then Trinity College, Cambridge, where he befriended Lord Byron and became known as the 'father of all mischiefs'.

He was first elected to Parliament in 1810 and did not make much of an impression; his maiden speech, according to fellow MP William Wellesley-Pole, was 'like a ranting whining bad actor in a barn speaking a full tragedy part, and mix'd up with the drawls and twangs of a Methodist preacher'. It was not a surprise, then, that he decided not to stand again two years later.

Instead, he decided to go travelling, and went to Spain to become an aide-de-camp to the Duke of Wellington during the Peninsular War. Once that was over, he stayed on the Continent, loitering and exploring. Colonel James Hamilton Stanhope encountered him in Porto around then, and later wrote: 'I never saw so singular a compound of eccentricity and judgement, of trifling and study; of sound opinions about others and wild speculations about himself, good talents applied to no future object and a most wonderful memory prostituted to old songs and tales of Mother Goose'.

After Europe came Egypt, Syria, Palestine and others. At the Great Temple of Ramses II in the former, he met Charles Barry, the architect who would go on to design the Palace of Westminster, and the pair struck up a lifelong friendship. He returned to England in 1820, by then a renowned traveller and collector. In the years that followed he was in and out of Parliament but seemingly without much enthusiasm, as there are few records of his achievements (or lack thereof) in the House of Commons.

In any case, an incident forced him to retreat from public life altogether in 1833, when he was caught getting frisky with a soldier in a urinal outside the Palace of Westminster. He denied the charges and got the Duke of Wellington and others to testify to his good character, and when the main witness left for America, he was acquitted.

Luckily, things picked up again in 1835 when he inherited his beloved family estate, Kingston Lacy in Dorset. By then an amateur architect (on top of everything else), he sought Barry's help and set out to transform the building, encasing the brick structure in stone and bringing the Philae obelisk over from Egypt.

Sadly, his troubles with the law were not over. In 1841 he was arrested for indecent behaviour again, this time with a guardsman – what is it with men in uniforms? – in Green Park. Realising that things were probably about to get dicey, he fled to France, was declared an outlaw, and eventually settled in Venice.

While there, he continued to furnish and embellish Kingston Lacy, buying paintings and commissioning sculptures, then sending them back to England, despite having been made to sign the estate over to his brother. Though he never returned to Britain and died in Italy, it is thought that he secretly went back to visit the family seat at least once; more than anything else, it was the love of his life.

Arthur MacMurrough Kavanagh (1831–89)

MP for County Wexford , 1866–8

MP for County Carlow, 1868–80

Arthur MacMurrough Kavanagh was born in County Carlow into one of the wealthiest families in Ireland at the time, and without arms or legs. Had he not been born into aristocracy, this probably would have been the end of this story, but luckily for him, the Kavanaghs had the means to adapt to his limblessness. Thanks to his mother and the nurse and doctor she hired, young Arthur started learning horse riding at the age of three, with the help of a special saddle.

In fact, he had a very active childhood, which included fishing, drawing, hunting, writing and anything else a young boy may dream of doing. If anything, he was probably having a bit too much fun; in 1849 his mother realised he had been rather busy fooling around with girls on the family estate, and sent him off to Sweden, then to Russia where his brother lived.

The young man probably did not mind as by that point he had already done some travelling of his own in Palestine and Egypt. Together, the brothers eventually left northern Europe and embarked on a journey through what are now India, Iran, Pakistan and Azerbaijan. To their mother's dismay,

Arthur kept doing what he did best, and spent at least two weeks in a harem while in India.

After his brother died, in 1851, he got himself hired as a despatch rider for the East India Company; after his other brother died, in 1853, he returned to Ireland to take care of the family business. After serving as a local high sheriff for a few years, Kavanagh stood for Parliament in 1866 and became the Tory MP for County Wexford.

The news of his election travelled far and wide, with Australian newspaper the *Brisbane Courier* noting in January 1867:

Mr. Kavanagh is descended from an ancient Irish family, and has a good patrimony, but it was his misfortune to be born without feet or hands – indeed he has but very short stumps in the place of either of his four limbs. He has a handsome face and robust body, with what is still more to the purpose, he has a quick and powerful mind, which has enabled him in a most wonderful manner to triumph over his sad physical disadvantages. He writes beautifully with his pen in his mouth, he is a good shot, a fair draftsman, and a dashing huntsman. He sits on horseback in a kind of saddle basket, and rides with great fearlessness.

He certainly made an impression in the Commons. He was allowed to prearrange interventions in debates with the Speaker because he could not wave his order paper to signal he wanted to speak, as MPs traditionally do, and had a manservant bring him into the Chamber and onto the Tory benches, who was then allowed to stay in the room. As for making his way from his constituency to London, he sailed to Parliament on his own yacht instead of taking a combination of train and ships, mooring just by the building itself.

On top of everything else, Kavanagh turned out to be a skilled parliamentarian. This is how his speech on the Poor Laws in Ireland was reported at the time:

. . . the right hon. gentleman in the chair, quietly nodding towards the Opposition benches said, 'Mr. Kavanagh.'

The effect of the words was electrical, and in an instant every eye in the House was turned towards the back seat, almost under the gallery, where the hon. member for Carlow sat, cool and collected, his papers arranged before him on his hat, and his face turned towards the chair. Opening his views in clear, well-chosen language, the hon. gentleman dived into his subject, and, in the course of a speech of some twelve minutes' duration, exhibited an intimate knowledge of the question under discussion which, as an extensive Irish landowner, he would naturally possess . . .

At the conclusion of his speech Mr. Kavanagh was loudly cheered. Judging by the matter of his first address, and the manner in which it was received, it may reasonably be predicted that Mr. Kavanagh, who belongs constitutionally to that type of men which wins in public life, the men with the large heads, deep chests, and faces full of force, will be often heard with advantage in the House of Commons.

After some years of honourable work in the Commons, Kavanagh came to be seen as the leader of the Irish Conservatives, which was unfortunate for him as the 1880 election marked the beginning of the Irish Parliamentary Party's dominance on the country's politics, and the year he lost his seat. He was not the most graceful of losers, marking the results by (somewhat dramatically) saying: 'the sting that rankles is the treachery and deceit of my own men, my own familiar friends in whom I trusted but that feeling must be choked'.

Still, his loss was a shock to many, and William Gladstone called him 'one of the ablest, if not the ablest, gentlemen coming from Ireland among the party opposite'. He was appointed lord lieutenant of County Carlow and invited to sit on the Bessborough Commission, which intended to improve relations between landlords and tenants, a topic close to Kavanagh's heart.

In 1886 he was appointed to the Privy Council of Ireland by Salisbury's government, which was more of an honorific title than anything else but must have been pleasing to receive nonetheless. Three years later, Kavanagh died of pneumonia on 25 December, peacefully listening to Christmas music.

Richard Barry (1769–93)

MP for Heytesbury, 1791–3

If you noticed the dates of birth and death above and wondered how much Richard Barry really could have done in that time, prepare to be impressed (and either worried or jealous, depending on how you believe one should lead one's life).

Born in a rich family in Middlesex, Richard Barry inherited his father's earldom at the age of three. His mother died when he was eleven, after which his grandmother, the Countess of Harrington, sent him off to Eton with £1,000 (over £150,000 today) in pocket money. He made good use of it, as once puberty hit, he would summon a cab driver to come to pick him up from school and take him to London brothels.

He enjoyed bets and pranks and became a friend of the boy who would eventually become George IV, but his real passions were hunting and the theatre. At eighteen he secured advances against his inheritance and bought a house in Berkshire, where he built stables and kept a pack of hounds.

Then, in 1788, he decided to build a theatre opposite his home, pouring £60,000 (nearly £10 million) into the project. It was a success at first; distinguished guests attended the opening night, and Barry made himself popular in the area by allowing the locals to attend the evening's entertainment for free.

To celebrate his twenty-first birthday he held a grand dinner and theatre performance, both attended by the Prince of Wales, and to celebrate his twenty-second he held a week-long party. By that point he had gained the nicknames Hellgate and Rake of Rakes, and was entirely predictably in debt.

Keen to find a way to escape his creditors, he did what any young man from a good family would do, and decided to stand for Parliament. At first it was Oxford, where he held a lavish dinner for his potential electors, including a soup made from a 150-pound turtle as the main dish. When that failed, he turned to the seat of Heytesbury in Wiltshire a year later, which he won. Though technically a Whig, not much is known of his time in Parliament, presumably because he did not spend much time there.

His ploy to become an MP in order to save his finances didn't work either, as his beloved theatre was destroyed and its contents sold in 1792. Still, at least he got married that summer – to a woman he loved but who was the daughter of a sedan chair man, and could not help him with his money troubles. At least the couple shared a mutual interest. Barry had been a boxing enthusiast and patron of a bare-knuckle boxer nicknamed Hooper the Tinman, and his wife Charlotte Goulding became a keen boxer herself, eventually being remembered as the Boxing Baroness.

Sadly, they never got to fight each other through to old age, as in 1793 Barry took a commission in the Berkshire militia and was sent off to Sussex. He was put in charge of escorting some French prisoners from Rye to Deal, which meant keeping a loaded rifle with him at all times. As should have been expected, he stopped at an inn for refreshments along the way, after which he managed to drop his rifle and shoot himself in the eye. He was dead less than an hour later; hadn't even reached twenty-five.

Sir William Paddy (1554–1634)

MP for Thetford, 1604–11

Born in London to a merchant family, William Paddy entered St John's College, Oxford, as a commoner in 1571, and in 1589 was admitted as a licentiate by the Royal College of Physicians back in his hometown. In 1596 he became a lecturer in anatomy and was given a licence to dissect corpses, one of only thirty-one doctors licensed by the Royal College to practise in London.

In 1603 James I became king of England and Ireland and appointed him as his physician, knighting him in Windsor in the process. A year later, Paddy became the MP for Thetford and turned into a reasonably active parliamentarian, serving on a wide range of committees and often speaking in the Chamber. All in all, everything was going well for Sir William Paddy. Indeed, everything kept going largely well for him as he became president of the Royal College of Physicians and kept serving the king as his physician.

Still, one hiccup took place in 1609, which is the reason why he is featured here. Paddy had welcomed Elizabeth Brydges, a courtier and former member of Elizabeth I's household, into his home. Some say she had been convalescing after a bout of ill health; others that she had moved out after finding out her husband was already married, and that the couple had separated.

In any case, her husband, Sir John Kennedy, one of the king's Scottish favourites and a notoriously violent man, did not take kindly to the move. This is what diplomat Dudley Carleton wrote about the night everything very nearly went pear-shaped for the physician and his (probable) mistress:

You have heard I am sure of a great danger Sir William Paddy lately escaped at Barn Elms, where the house was assaulted by Sir John Kennedy by night with a band of furious Scots, who besides their warlike weapons came furnished . . . with certain snippers and searing irons, purposing to have used him worse than a Jew, with much more ceremony than circumcision. Sir William, having the alarm given him, fled like a valiant knight out at a back door, leaving his breaches [*sic*] behind him, and the lady by his sweet side went tripping over the plains in her smock with her petticoat in her hand till they recovered the next castle.

It just goes to show; you may be one of the most distinguished doctors in the country, but sleep with someone else's wife and you may well end up running away from your castle as furious Scots try to chop off your genitals. And that is, frankly, all there is to say about Sir William Paddy.

5

The Outlaws and the Villains

Such exotic and convoluted conspiratorial activity that it seemed impossible to disentangle truth from rumor, propaganda stunts or psychological warfare.

Bernard Wasserstein on the life of
Ignaz Trebitsch-Lincoln

Noel Pemberton-Billing (1881–1948)

MP for Hertford, 1916–21

It is hard to decide which category Noel Pemberton-Billing belongs to. Is he a villain? An adventurer? An eccentric? Perhaps he really did manage to be all three in the end. So let's start at the beginning – it may be easier to let you decide for yourself.

The son of an iron founder from Birmingham, Noel Pemberton-Billing was born in Hampstead, London, but was clearly desperate to leave it from a young age. At thirteen he set fire to his headmaster's office, ran away from home and stowed away on a ship headed for South Africa. Once there, he did a series of menial jobs, became a boxer, did some acting and eventually joined the British Army at eighteen and went to fight in the Second Boer War. By 1901 he had been invalided out of the army after getting wounded twice, and by 1903 he was back in Britain, where he opened a garage in Kingston upon Thames. Cars weren't his real passion, however; planes were. What followed was a bit of a professional mixed bag, as Billing tried to open an aerodrome in Essex but failed, was briefly in property, studied law but then decided to sell steam yachts instead, and tried to found a flying field in 1909, which sadly didn't take off either.

Undeterred, he bet the industrialist Frederick Handley Page £500 – around £60,000 today – that he could earn a pilot's licence within twenty-four hours of sitting in an aircraft for the first time. The bet was won after he spent an impressively short 'four hours and two minutes in the air'. He used the money to launch Pemberton-Billing Limited, an aircraft business, and soon set out to work on designing a flying boat, alongside other machines. That didn't go very far, but it didn't matter. By 1914 the First World War had broken out, and he bagged a temporary commission as a lieutenant in the Royal Navy Air Service, then sold his shares in the company two years later. Though he would brag about all he had done during the war and claimed to have risen to the rank of squadron commander, according to military historian James Hayward, 'Later, official sources would claim that Billing had spent only 12 months in the RNAS, had never flown on a raid or in the face of the enemy, and never rose beyond Flight Lieutenant.'

In fact, 1916 became a major turning point in Pemberton-Billing's life. In January he tried to stand for Parliament in Mile End as an independent candidate, and though his claim that the area needed a 'proper airman' to protect it from German Zeppelins was popular, he lost to the Conservative candidate. Clearly keen to get in one way or another, he then stood for Hertfordshire in a by-election three months later, which he won. The same year he founded and started editing the *Imperialist*, a weekly journal partly funded by Lord Beaverbrook, and which he mostly used to promote his parliamentary campaigns.

Though some of those were admirable – equal votes for men and women was one of them – most weren't. By 1917, Pemberton-Billing had succumbed to paranoia and thought Britain had been overrun by secret German sympathisers and other assorted traitors. These included, among others, Fabians, internationalists, immigrants and – sadly unsurprisingly – Jewish people, but he soon had a certain community in his sights. In December 1917, the *Imperialist* published a piece by Arnold Henry White which claimed:

> Espionage is punished by death at the Tower of London, but there is a form of invasion which is as deadly as espionage: the systematic seduction of young British soldiers by the German urnings [homosexuals] and their agents . . . Failure to intern all Germans is due to the invisible hand that protects urnings of enemy race . . . When the blond beast is an urning, he commands the urnings in other lands. They are moles. They burrow. They plot. They are hardest at work when they are most silent.

Pemberton-Billing spoke frequently in the Chamber that year – especially on matters relating to air warfare, earning the nickname Minister for Air – but his obsession with the idea that gay men and women were helping the Germans did not wane. In February 1918 he renamed his magazine the *Vigilante* after his (ultimately unsuccessful) campaign to set up a Vigilance Committee of nine independent politicians to oversee the government in the Commons. He also published another piece on the 'Unseen Hand', which he remained convinced was working against Britain, this time by spreading venereal diseases on purpose:

The German, through his efficient and clever agent, the Ashkenazim, has complete control of the White Slave Traffic. Germany has found that diseased women cause more casualties than bullets. Controlled by their Jew-agents, Germany maintains in Britain a self-supporting – even profit-making – army of prostitutes which put more men out of action than does their army of soldiers.

While this was all rather extreme, it was still only the tip of the iceberg as far as he was concerned. The real secret, according to the *Vigilante*, was the Black Book. In January they had told their readers about the existence, 'in the Cabinet Noir of a certain German Prince, [of] a book compiled by the Secret Service from reports of German agents who have infested this country for the past twenty years, agents so vile and spreading such debauchery and such lasciviousness as only German minds can conceive and only German bodies execute'.

Among those 47,000 (!) traitors were 'Privy Councillors, youths of the chorus, wives of Cabinet Ministers, dancing girls, even Cabinet Ministers themselves . . . diplomats, poets, bankers, editors, newspaper proprietors'.

It all came to a head a month later when Pemberton-Billing and his fellow travellers were made aware of a play about to be performed in London. It had it all: the theatrical producer was Jack Grein, a Dutchman educated in Germany; the actress was Maud Allan, a Canadian woman who had studied in Berlin; and the play was *Salome* by Oscar Wilde, which had been banned by Lord Chamberlain for being blasphemous. As a result the two performances were to be private and kept a secret. The MP was convinced that Allan was having an affair with Margot Asquith, the wife of former PM Herbert, and thought that all three were members of the Unseen Hand – because of course he did.

This led to the *Vigilante* splashing 'The Cult of the Clitoris'* on its front page on 16 February, where the paper explained: 'To be a member of Maud Allan's private performances in Oscar Wilde's *Salome* one has to apply to a Miss Valetta, of 9 Duke Street, Adelphi, W.C. If Scotland Yard were to seize the list of those members I have no doubt they would secure the names of several of the first 47,000.'

Though she did happen to be a bona fide lesbian, Allan decided to risk it and sue Billing for obscene, criminal and defamatory libel. The court case was, to put it mildly, a mess. Billing represented himself and tried to throw everything he could at Allan, and the two witnesses who appeared to say they had seen the Black Book were his mistress Eileen Villiers-Stewart and Harold Spencer, a *Vigilante* writer who'd been dismissed from the army for 'paranoid delusional insanity'. Billing was somehow acquitted of all charges, and crowds cheered at the news outside the courtroom; meanwhile, Allan was eventually forced to leave the country and settle in the United States with her partner.

Still, there is some justice in the world, as this ended up being the high point of Pemberton-Billing's career. His popularity post court case allowed him to get re-elected after the war, but there was no longer any appetite for his conspiracy

---

* An amusing side note to this is that most men hadn't even heard of the word 'clitoris' at the time, so though presumably not what he had in mind, Noel Pemberton-Billing at least contributed to a more widespread understanding of female genitalia.

theories. Then there was Villiers-Stewart's admission in late 1918 that she'd lied in court about the Black Book, and Spencer's conviction for criminal libel in 1920 for an anti-Semitic pamphlet he'd written about Churchill conspiring with Jewish traitors to kill Lord Kitchener. Billing left Parliament a year later.

Though he became largely irrelevant in the interwar period, he did gain some publicity during the Second World War for trying and failing to re-enter Parliament on a platform of, among other things, creating a 'woman's Parliament' to deal with issues in the home. His death in 1948 was barely noted.

Orlando Bridgeman (1678–1746)

MP for Coventry, 1707–10

MP for Calne, 1715–22

MP for Lostwithiel, 1724–7

MP for Bletchingley, 1727–34

MP for Dunwich, 1734–8

Things started pretty well for Orlando Bridgeman; he was the grandson of Charles II's Lord Keeper, and succeeded to his father's estates and baronetcy at the age of twenty-three. A year later he married the daughter of Sir Francis Dashwood, a wealthy merchant, and as a result acquired a manor in Essex. In 1705 he stood for Parliament as a Whig, lost, contested the result and managed to reverse it, then became the MP for Coventry in 1707. The following twenty-three years he spent in the Commons (with some interruptions) were neither impressive nor pitiful; at his height he was a lord of trade on the Board of Trade.

Still, things started to go downhill in the late 1730s. Bridgeman had been building a new house on his family's Bowood estate, in Wiltshire, and costs were mounting, pushing him further and further into debt. By 1737 the Chancery Courts had begun proceedings against him, the same year he had been nominated as governor of Barbados, a lucrative albeit dangerous position.

He was due to leave for the island in 1738 but killed himself before the ship could sail, having left some letters for the king and his family. His clothes were left on the shore of the Thames, and on 10 June a badly disfigured corpse turned up in the river and was assumed to be his. Bridgeman was declared dead and his son Francis inherited the baronetcy.

Sadly for Bridgeman junior, some had doubts about his father's passing, and a reward was offered to anyone who could find him. The move was a shrewd one; in October 1739 Bridgeman was found alive and healthy in an inn in Gloucester and summarily sent to prison there, where he died in 1746. Tragically, poor Francis had also passed away by that point, so never got to re-inherit the title.

John Stubbs (1544?–90?)

MP for Great Yarmouth, 1589

Born in Norfolk, John Stubbs was educated at Trinity College, Cambridge, graduating in 1564 and entering Lincoln's Inn a year later, and getting called to the Bar in 1572. At some point during those years he developed some strong puritan views, which would soon land him in trouble.

In 1579 it was announced that Queen Elizabeth I was to marry Francis, Duke of Anjou, who was not only a Roman Catholic but also a foreigner and the brother of the king of France. Outraged, Stubbs wrote a pamphlet arguing against the union, snappily titled *The Discovery of a Gaping Gulf whereunto England is like to be swallowed by another French Marriage, if the Lord forbid not the banns, by letting her Majesty see the sin and punishment thereof*. In it, he called the proposed marriage 'contrary coupling', 'an immoral union' and 'an uneven yoking of the clean ox to the unclean ass', adding that the duke's family clearly suffered from venereal diseases and that given Elizabeth's advanced age, she probably couldn't have children anyway.

Word of the pamphlet soon spread and, as you can imagine, did not go down well in royal circles. In September 1579 a royal proclamation was issued which prohibited circulation of the book, and a few weeks later Stubbs, his printer Hugh Singleton and distributer William Page were arrested. Though Queen Elizabeth originally wanted the three men to be executed by royal prerogative, the case went to trial and they were convicted of sedition. Singleton was eventually pardoned – probably due to his advanced age – but Stubbs and Page were sentenced to having their right hands cut off.

Either remorseful or keen to keep his arm intact, Stubbs wrote to the queen to apologise, somewhat pathetically calling himself the 'sorrowfullest man in the world' and explaining that his 'poor heart never conceived malicious thought or wicked purpose'. Though certainly worth a shot, it failed to change the queen's mind, and on 3 November the pair went to meet their fate.

According to contemporary writer William Camden,

> Stubbs and Page had their right hands cut off with a cleaver, driven through the wrist by the force of a mallet, upon a scaffold in the marketplace at Westminster . . . I remember that Stubbs, after his right hand was cut off, took off his hat with his left, and said with a loud voice, 'God Save the Queen'; the crowd standing about was deeply silent: either out of horror at this new punishment; or else out of sadness.

Stubbs then fainted, and was carried to the Tower of London to serve his custodial sentence.

Sadly for Elizabeth, the move had turned out to be the wrong one; public opinion was by that point firmly against her and the union, and in 1580 she announced that the marriage would not be taking place. Stubbs, meanwhile, was released from prison a year later and kept writing pamphlets, although managing to stay out of trouble. In 1585 he took his first steps in public life by becoming the steward of Great Yarmouth, and in 1589 he became the area's MP. He used the platform to once again state his support for the queen, despite what she had done to his hand, once ending a speech with the panegyric:

> In health of your person, in honour of your name, in joy of your heart, and in all flourishing happiness . . . We shall . . . employ the services of our goods, bodies, lives and all our means whatsoever [on your behalf] . . .

[both] in regard to our natural allegiance and for the infinite graces which we enjoy by you . . . [May] God . . . bless your Majesty and curse all those that say not thereto 'Amen'.

This ending was a happy but short-lived one, as he died a year later while volunteering for military service – in France, of all places. And if this isn't bittersweet enough for your liking – here is what he wrote in his will:

I protest and contest that I lived and do die the true man and most loyal subject of her most excellent Majesty Elizabeth, by God's singular grace our happy Queen, beseeching her most merciful and royal nature that after my death my most true and well-deserving wife, mine executrix, may find that grace and favour in her Majesty's eyes which, though I could not deserve, I yet would have esteemed for a great blessing on earth.

John Sadleir (1813–56)

MP for Carlow, 1847–53

MP for Sligo Borough, 1853–6

Disappointingly for someone later nicknamed the Prince of Swindlers, John Sadleir's life was not a very happy one. Born in County Tipperary in Ireland, he was the third son of a tenant farmer and his maternal grandfather was the founder of a local private bank. He qualified as a solicitor and took over a successful practice from his uncle in Dublin, but decided to leave law behind in 1846 to pursue a career in banking.

He soon managed to become a chairman and director of several banks and some railway companies, and got elected as the MP for Carlow in 1847. In 1852 he was one of the leading figures of the newly created Independent Irish Party, which briefly held the balance of power in the House of Commons. The party had managed to bring down the Tory ministry of Lord Derby and got Peelite Lord Aberdeen and the Whigs to form a coalition. However, despite having been elected on a platform of not taking office, Sadleir accepted the post of junior lord of the Treasury.

This caused widespread outrage in Ireland, but his career on the front bench did not last long anyway. In 1854 he resigned after being found guilty of taking part in a plot to imprison a depositor of the Tipperary Joint Stock Bank who had not voted for him. This was only the tip of the iceberg; the bank had been launched by Sadleir, his brother James and their cousin James Scully a few years previously, and was about to cause their downfall.

You see, Sadleir had been busy speculating in gold companies, land and railway stocks, commodities and coal mines, and losing a tremendous amount of money in the process. In order to sustain his hobby, he had been borrowing more and more money from several banks, including the Tipperary. Then, presumably realising that he was already in for a penny, he started embezzling trust assets and stealing title deeds, selling counterfeit shares and forging bills of exchange. On top of that, he also brought a small bank in Newcastle-upon-Tyne to ruin and sold forged shares of the Swedish Railway Company.

By February 1856 he had amassed an overdraft of £288,000 at the Tipperary Bank – tens of millions in today's money – causing the bank to become insolvent. Feeling that there was no way out of the hole he'd dug for himself, John Sadleir went to Hampstead Heath on 17 February, drank a bottle of prussic acid, and died on the spot.

His legacy was not a resplendent one, his name remaining a shorthand for 'turncoat' in Irish politics for decades after his death. Still, he was the inspiration for Mr Merdle in *Little Dorrit* by Charles Dickens, and more generally, the real person behind countless fictional characters going bankrupt, then killing themselves.

James Sadleir (1815–81)

MP for Tipperary, 1852–7

There is no point going through the early years of James Sadleir as they are very similar to his brother's; born in County Tipperary, grandson of a local banker, co-founded the Tipperary Bank – you know the drill. Sadleir entered Parliament a few years after his brother as a Liberal MP, but didn't make any waves while there – until the events of early 1856, that is.

Before killing himself, John sent a letter to his brother's wife that read as follows:

James is not to blame – I alone have caused all this dreadful ruin. James was to me too fond a brother but he is not to blame for being deceived and led astray by my diabolical acts. Be to him at this moment all the support you can. Oh what I would not suffer with gladness to save those whom I have ruined. My end will prove at least that I was not callous to their agony.

It was a valiant effort, and it worked for a while. As creditors started suing the bank to recover their money, Sadleir was painted by the press as a figure of pity who had to deal with the failures of his no-good brother. This didn't last long. Court inquiries soon started disclosing troubling documents, including correspondence between the two brothers showing that James had known more than he'd let on.

Presumably realising that things weren't looking good for him, James fled the country on 17 June 1856, confirming his guilt in the process. Charges were brought against him *in absentia* a month later, but no one knew where he had absconded to. There were rumours of sightings in New Orleans and South America, but nothing conclusive.

It all changed in February 1857 when MPs debated expelling Sadleir from the House of Commons and John FitzGerald read out a very dramatic letter he'd received a few days earlier:

Hotel du Louvre, rue de Rivoli, Paris, Feb. 12, 1857.

Sir,— I consider it my duty to inform you that the notorious culprit James Sadleir is now in Paris, having seen him last night enter a restaurant in the Palace Royal, where I dined, and having caught my eye, he immediately withdrew.

The proprietor, M. Dupuis, afterwards informed

me that he dines there every day. If the Government is anxious to arrest him, by sending over persons acquainted with his personal appearance, the object can be attained. His countenance is much altered; having lost his flesh and colour, and also wearing a moustache, a considerable change has taken place.

This information shall be kept secret by me until I receive your reply.

I remain your obedient servant,
James Scully.

As you may remember, Scully was the brothers' cousin who had been involved in setting up the bank. He clearly felt that he'd been swindled by the pair as well. Though his letter did not result in Sadleir getting arrested, as his crimes didn't fulfil the criteria of the extradition treaty between the two countries, James Sadleir did get expelled from the House of Commons that week.

Three months later he attempted to clear his name, not by coming back from self-imposed exile – that would just be silly – but by sending a letter to the *Dublin Evening Post*. In it, he explained that he hadn't known about his brother's dodgy speculations, and that he had 'denounced him in the strongest language' after finding out. To say that reactions to the letter were mixed would be too kind, as, to pick one example of many, Dublin's *Freeman's Journal* called him a 'felon, who should now be working in a chain gang, instead of enjoying the luxuries of Paris'.

Unable to redeem himself, Sadleir continued his life on the Continent in Switzerland, first in Geneva, then in Zurich. It was there that, in 1881, he encountered a thief intent on stealing his gold watch. He resisted and, as a result, was shot to death. His body was found a week later, hidden in a thicket.

Charles Bradlaugh (1833–91)

MP for Northampton, 1880–91

One of seven children, Charles Bradlaugh was the son of a solicitor's clerk and was brought up in Hoxton, east London. He left school at eleven to be an office boy at his father's company, then became a Sunday school teacher, but didn't stay on for long. A curious young man, Bradlaugh had concerns about the Scriptures, which he took to his local vicar. This turned out to be a mistake, as it saw him accused of 'atheism', suspended from teaching and eventually thrown out of the family home, all while still a teenager.

He was taken in by Eliza Sharples Carlile, the widow of political agitator and freethinker Richard Carlile. These would turn out to be his most formative years, as she introduced him to the radical ideas of her former husband and his clique – equality between the sexes, contraception, atheism – and it is around then that he met prominent secularist George Holyoake.

Though well on his way to becoming a freethinker, Bradlaugh decided to enlist in the army in 1850, joining the 7th Dragoon Guards and getting posted to Ireland. The stint was relatively short-lived, as his father died in 1852 and by 1853 he used a legacy he'd inherited from his great aunt to purchase his discharge. Back in London, he took up a job as an errand boy, then clerk to solicitor Thomas Rogers, and soon got married to a woman named Susannah Lamb Hooper.

By that point his ideas and convictions had become his main focus, and he was keeping himself busy writing pamphlets on secularism under the pen name 'Iconoclast' and getting close to radical and liberal groups. In 1860 he co-launched the *National Reformer*, a newspaper campaigning for atheistic secularism, republicanism and universal suffrage. In 1865 he teamed up with a number of members from the International Workingmen's Association and established the Reform League, which aimed to campaign for one man, one vote. A year after that he co-founded the National Secular Society, becoming close to campaigner Annie Besant in the process.

Doing this much in only a few years was impressive, but it soon got him into trouble. In 1868 the *National Reformer* was prosecuted by the government for blasphemy and sedition, but Bradlaugh was eventually acquitted of all charges. Eight years later, in 1876, he and Besant published *The Fruits of Philosophy; or, The Private Companion of Young Married People*, a pamphlet advocating for birth control written by American atheist Charles Knowlton. Unsurprisingly, as the previous publishers had been sued before them, the pair were charged with publishing material 'likely to deprave or corrupt those whose minds are open to immoral influences'. Though found guilty of 'obscene libel' and sentenced to six months in prison, their conviction was later overturned at the Court of Appeal, and the whole saga led to the founding of the Malthusian League, which campaigned for contraception and family planning.

Still, all these battles were only a warm-up for the biggest fight in Bradlaugh's life, which started in 1880 when he was elected as the new Liberal MP for Northampton. In order to actually take up his seat, he needed to take the (religious) Oath of Allegiance, which, as you can imagine, he wasn't particularly keen on doing. Instead, he decided to use the event as an opportunity to show that 'atheists were held to be incapable of taking a meaningful oath, and were therefore treated as outlaws'.

Citing the Evidence Amendment Acts of 1869 and 1870, he went up to the Table of the House of Commons and asked to be able to affirm instead of take the oath. It went about as well as could be expected; unwilling to take a decision himself, the Speaker asked the House to decide for him, and a special select committee was set up to explore the question. After one brief meeting on 12 May, said committee decided that Bradlaugh could not affirm instead of taking the oath. Seemingly defeated, Bradlaugh announced that he would simply have to take the oath if there were no other options, but did so by writing an open letter to *The Times*, published on 21 May, in which he noted the oath did include 'words of idle and meaningless character'.

This was, you will once again be shocked to hear, a self-defeating move. When Bradlaugh went to take the oath he'd openly mocked in a newspaper, MPs objected to it in the Chamber, making the House set up another select committee to decide whether an MP could be stopped from taking the oath. In an amusing plot twist, it found that while the House could 'and, in the opinion of your Committee, ought to' prevent him from taking the oath, Bradlaugh should in fact try to affirm instead in order to try and clarify the law on the topic. Unhappy with this development, his fellow

MPs voted in an amendment forbidding him both from taking the oath and making an affirmation.

When Bradlaugh tried to come into the Chamber the next day to finally do the bloody thing, he was made to withdraw by the Speaker, and instead gave his maiden speech from behind the Bar, which is physically inside the Chamber but considered to be out of it. In it, he argued that he should be allowed to take the oath as he had not been legally disqualified from it, which was a fair enough point but didn't change enough hearts or minds. A motion was passed forcing Bradlaugh to withdraw, which he refused to do, and after some back and forth he was brought into custody by the serjeant-at-arms.

Fearing that keeping him in there would only make him a martyr, then Conservative leader Benjamin Disraeli successfully argued that he should be released. This brief spell in prison did not dampen Bradlaugh's spirits. In 1881 he tried to take his seat once more and even participated in a vote, which saw him removed from the House of Commons. A by-election was held in Northampton, and he won it. In 1882 he presented a petition signed by nearly a quarter of a million people calling for him to be able to take his seat, then tried to take his oath and was removed from the House of Commons again.

In 1883 William Gladstone tried to bring forward an Affirmation Bill, which would have done what it said on the tin, but it was defeated. In 1884 Bradlaugh was elected as the MP for Northampton again, and managed to vote three times before getting excluded, later getting a £1,500 fine for having voted illegally. Determined to get his way, he stood (again) in Northampton (again) in 1886 and won (again), then went to take his oath (again), but this time things were different. Sir Arthur Wellesley Peel, the new Speaker of the House of Commons, decided that it would not be his place to interfere in the oath-taking, and so Bradlaugh was finally able to become a bona fide serving member of Parliament.

Sadly, his parliamentary career didn't last long, as he passed away under five years later. Still, he had by that point managed to help secure the passing of the Oaths Act 1888, allowing MPs to solemnly affirm their oath as well as swearing it to God, and ensuring that he got the last laugh.

John Stonehouse (1925–88)

MP for Wednesbury, 1957–74

MP for Walsall North, 1974–6

John Stonehouse had exactly the upbringing you may expect from a bog standard left-wing politician. He was born in Southampton and joined the Labour Party at the age of sixteen; his mother was a councillor on Southampton City Council and the mayor of Southampton for some time, and his father a trade unionist. He attended a local college, then moved to London to study at the London School of Economics.

After being conscripted for a two-year stint in the RAF, he became an economist and joined various co-operative movements. Keen to get into politics, he tried and failed to get a seat on the London County Council in 1949, a parliamentary seat in Twickenham a year later, and another one in

Burton a year after that. Things started looking up in 1956 when he became the director of the London Co-operative Society, then in 1957 when he was finally elected as the Labour Co-operative MP for Wednesbury.

It was all going well. In 1959 he went to Rhodesia and spoke at the Southern Rhodesia African National Congress, where he encouraged the black majority to rise up, telling them that they had the support of his party to do so.

Then came 1962, which proved to be a turning point for Stonehouse. On the one hand, he became the president of the London Co-operative Society; on the other, he started spying for Czechoslovakia.

In 1964 he became a junior minister for aviation, and was allegedly paid £5,000 – over £100,000 in today's money – to pass on details on what was going on in his department. He was promoted to minister of state for technology in 1967, then to Postmaster General a year later, where he introduced the first- and second-class mail system. He was also appointed to the Privy Council that same year, which was, for obvious reasons, less than ideal. His gradual rise was put to a sharp end in 1969, when former Czech spy turned defector Josef Frolik (great name) outed Stonehouse as a fellow spy to the security services.

He was questioned twice by MI5's Cold War officer Charles Elwell and in front of then Prime Minister Harold Wilson, but somehow managed to successfully deny all allegations. This got him out of the pan, but unfortunately fire was still awaiting. In 1970 Labour lost the general election and Stonehouse found himself on the back benches, without the additional income he had got as a minister and with Wilson still clinging on to the leadership, so with no hope of joining the shadow cabinet. This also meant that the tips he got from Czechoslovakia had dried up, and he soon found himself in need of extra cash.

At first, Stonehouse tried to get himself some more funds through legal means by setting up a number of businesses in different countries, including an investment bank in Bangladesh. Sadly, these all failed and he found himself in debt for millions of pounds in today's money. By 1974 he had started forging documents and resorting to creative accounting with the help of his secretary and lover Sheila Buckley. Aware that the Department of Trade and Industry was starting to look into him, he decided to start plotting his exit that year.

The plan was organised months in advance. He picked the name Joseph Markham, which had been that of the dead husband of one of his constituents, and had been rehearsing his new identity. On 20 November he left a pile of his clothes on a beach in Miami and flew to Australia with Buckley, assuming the name of Clive Mildoon, another dead constituent. Meanwhile, back home, it was assumed that Stonehouse had drowned or been attacked by a shark; obituaries were published, and a ceremonial service was held in the House of Commons.

His plan had worked perfectly, and it is fair to say that he almost certainly would have got away with it if it hadn't been for one pesky disgraced politician. Two weeks before Stonehouse's 'death', Lord Lucan had also absconded. While the former was not a priority as debts were the only things he had left behind, the latter's disappearance had involved a dead nanny and an injured wife. The hunt for Lucan was on, and so when Scotland Yard was told of a wealthy-seeming British man operating under two names and moving large sums of money between banks in Australia, its interest was piqued.

Then, when investigators realised their suspect was reading newspaper stories about dead MP John Stonehouse, they knew they had another fugitive on their hands. Still, they had to be sure, and so when Markham/Mildoon was apprehended on Christmas Eve, he was made to drop his trousers, since Lucan was known to have a large scar on his inner right thigh. After trying and failing to get asylum in Mauritius and Sweden, Stonehouse was deported to Britain six months later. He was remanded in Brixton Prison, all the while still managing to remain a Labour MP. Released on bail in August 1975, he even gave a speech in the House of Commons in which he pleaded: 'I assumed a new parallel personality that took over from me, which was foreign to me and which despised the humbug and sham of the past years of my public life.'

When his trial came in 1976, he conducted his own defence on twenty-one charges of fraud, theft, forgery, conspiracy to defraud, causing a false police investigation and wasting police time, and on 7 August was sentenced to seven years in prison. He finally resigned from Parliament in the same month, having' by that point become an English National Party MP. In August 1979 he was released early from prison because of good behaviour and poor health.

Still interested in politics, he joined the SDP and spent his last few years writing novels and appearing on television and radio, mostly to discuss the faking of his death. His real death came in 1988, when he collapsed on set during the filming of a show about missing people.

Ignaz Trebitsch-Lincoln (1879–1943)

MP for Darlington, 1910

How are you reading this book? Is it in large chunks, swallowing biography after biography, or only one MP at a time, when you have a moment? If it is the latter, you may want to set some time aside for this one, as it will be longer than the others – and for good reason; Ignaz Trebitsch-Lincoln got a lot more done in his time than the others. Not that he really left his mark on history. If you have heard of him, you are the exception. Still, his story is worth telling in some detail, as . . . well, you'll see.

Ignacz Trebitsch was born in the small town of Paks in Hungary into an Orthodox Jewish family. After leaving school, he studied to become an actor at the Royal Hungarian Academy of Dramatic Art in Budapest, but dropped out twice. As his father's business was collapsing, he got in some trouble with the police over some petty thefts, and in 1897 he left the country and ended up in London. While there, he joined some Christian missionaries and became a convert, getting baptised on 24 December 1899. He then set off to study at a Lutheran seminary in Germany, but not before stealing jewellery from the wife of the Reverend Lypshytz, the man who'd converted him and who would later describe him as 'thoroughly bad, a genius, and very attractive, but taking the crooked way always for choice'.

After growing restless in the seminary, Trebitsch was sent off to Canada as a missionary, tasked with trying to convert members of the Jewish community in Montreal, first for the Presbyterians, then the Anglicans. He failed to convert a

single one, then went back to Britain in 1903 after an argu-
ment over his stipend. In the last act of his ecclesiastical
career, he became acquainted with the Archbishop of
Canterbury, which helped him bag a post as a curate in
Kent. While there, he met confectionery and cocoa millionaire and Quaker Seebohm Rowntree, who was a prominent
figure in the Liberal Party, and Rowntree made him his
private secretary. Thanks to this post, he led a lavish life
across Europe and would often pester the Foreign Office to
help him gather documents from foreign embassies, which
was the start of a long and tortuous relationship between
the man and the department – but more on that later.

After securing British naturalisation in May 1909, Timothy
Trebich-Lincoln, as he was then known, convinced Rowntree
to lend him £10,000 – over £1 million today – and use his
connections in the party to get him nominated as a Liberal
candidate for the upcoming election. In January 1910 (and
after some strategic lying about the date of his naturalisation),
he beat Darlington's sitting Tory MP Pike Pease, and celebrated the victory by gloating: 'They have brought out a
poster in Darlington – "The foreigner's got my job." Well,
he has got it. I am the foreigner; I have got Pike Pease's
job.'

Immediately afterwards, he travelled to Hungary to show
off to his parents about his new job and, among other things,
deliver a speech claiming that the Liberal Party did not
support independence from Austro-Hungary.

There is not much to say about the time he spent in
Parliament after that, as it was very short; members were
not paid at the time and he was already having troubles with
his finances when he was elected, so when another election

was called later that same year, he decided not to stand again. It also probably did not help that the Foreign Office had caught wind of his freelance speech-making abroad, and was not overly pleased about it.

This left him with no job, no money and a wife and children to feed, so he turned to business. In 1911 he started the Amalgamated Oil Pipe-Lines of Galicia, which would have been more successful if oil in Galicia hadn't hit its peak two years previously. As this venture was about to fail for good in 1912, he set up the Oil and Drilling Trust of Roumania, which didn't get off to a great start as he was milking it from the beginning but which became untenable when Romania got caught in the Balkan Wars in 1913.

Penniless once more, he returned to England, took up a poorly paid job as a censor in the War Office and lived in a boarding house with his family. Things swiftly went down-hill as he admitted to Rowntree – remember him? – that he'd been forging letters of guarantee from him in order to get loans, hoping to be forgiven. Instead, Rowntree reported him to the man who'd loaned him money, and Scotland Yard was soon on the case. At around the same time, a Romanian court convicted him *in absentia* of misappropri-ation of money and goods from the Oil and Drilling Trust of Roumania, and sentenced him to a hefty fine and seven months in prison.

Things then took an odd turn. Realising he was about to be in trouble, Trebitsch-Lincoln went to MO5 (soon to become MI5) and offered to spy on the Germans for them. His plan was to go to the Netherlands and report on what the Germans were doing there. It was very predictably rejected by MO5. He decided to go to Rotterdam anyway, where he met the German consul general and – plot twist – got a freelance gig spying on French and British ships and harbours for Germany.

After doing that for a few months, he went back to Britain and tried to sell whatever he had gleaned from the Germans back to Britain, but was turned down. Aware that things were not looking good for him in Europe by that point, he left his family behind and jumped on a ship bound for New York (on which he managed to seduce two German sisters, but that's off-topic). Once there, he reinvented himself again, this time as a much more important and thrilling version of the man he had been those past few years. He decided to tell his (somewhat embellished) story to the *New York World* newspaper, which headlined it 'Revelation of I. T. T. Lincoln, Former Member of Parliament Who Became a Spy'.

Unsurprisingly, gloating about having spied on Britain for the Germans was not really the done thing in the middle of a world war, and Trebitsch-Lincoln was arrested and thrown into a Brooklyn jail in 1915. While managing to delay his extradition, he admitted to having been a German spy but denied accusations of fraud. Then, in a very embarrassing turn of events for American intelligence, he wrote to the Bureau of Investigation (which would later become the FBI) to tell them he could help decipher German cables. Somehow they believed him, and gave him some time and space to crack some codes. As surely as could have been expected, Trebitsch-Lincoln used the opportunity to escape from custody, but was quickly caught, then finally deported to Britain.

Because we all need to switch it up a bit once in a while, his court appearance in England featured him going for the opposite of his American performance, by admitting to forgery but denying all charges of treason. Nevertheless, he was sentenced to three years in prison, which he served on the Isle of Wight, and had his British nationality revoked by the Home Secretary in 1918. After getting released in 1919, he was deported by ship to the Netherlands, and though he was assumed to be going back to his native Hungary, he stopped by in Germany instead.

Broken by the aftermath of the war and the Treaty of Versailles, the Weimar Republic was the ideal place for him to bloom. Bitter about the way he had been treated in London, he managed to sell a couple of anti-British stories to *Deutsche Zeitung*, a newspaper run by far-right nationalist and violent extremist Reinhold Wulle. Unusually, given Trebitsch-Lincoln's Jewish heritage, he managed to find a patron in Wulle, kept writing for the paper, and got involved in planning for the upcoming Kapp Putsch. The attempt to replace the republic with an autocratic and nationalist government took place on 13 March 1920, and the Freikorps swiftly managed to take control of Berlin.

Since it did not look like its success would extend beyond the city, few were keen to join the power grab, which allowed Trebitsch-Lincoln to become the press secretary of the Kapp government. Though the whole thing was short-lived – Wolfgang Kapp himself resigned on 17 March – it allowed our protagonist to briefly meet Adolf Hitler, which feels worth noting. In the scramble to leave after the fall of Kapp, he found himself associated with the White International, an anti-communist, anti-Semitic pro-monarchist group counting Gyula Gömbös, later to become Hungary's fascist prime minister, as one of its members. The organisation failed to get much done and disbanded fairly quickly, but Trebitsch-Lincoln still managed to steal their documents, flee to Austria and attempt to sell them on.

Though Britain, France and the US didn't take the bait, the Czechoslovak government did, and paid him handsomely for the files. In late 1920 they managed to get a three-part series published in *The Times* based on the dossier, in an attempt to turn public opinion against Hungary. The good news for Czechoslovakia was that the story was picked up by the press in several other countries; the bad news for Trebitsch-Lincoln was that it widely publicised the part he had played in the White International. He fled once more, this time to Vienna, but in 1921 he was arrested and brought to court by the Czechoslovak government for – somewhat confusingly – fraud and high treason, based on the documents he had sold them.

He managed not to get convicted and headed to Italy after his release, boarding a ship for the US from there. Clearly at ease on long journeys at sea, he used the opportunity to scam millionaire Albert Otto out of £15,000 (over £600,000 today), which should have set him up nicely in his new American life. Sadly, he was arrested in New York two months later for surreptitiously entering the country, told to leave at once, and somehow made his way to China in 1922. This really should have been the end of the story, given his lack of contacts in the country, but somehow – heaven knows how, really – he managed to make it work.

One way or another, he found employment working for successive warlords, including Sichuan-based Yang Sen. In 1923 he travelled to Europe to raise funds for Ch'i

Hsieh-yuan, another warlord, and was reunited with his family in the process. The mission, however, turned into a failure, and fearing retributions, Trebitsch-Lincoln fled to present-day Indonesia with his wife and children. After a brief spell trying and failing to win big at baccarat in Monte Carlo, he abandoned his family once more and went back to New York to do what he did best: in this case, selling embellished stories of his time in China to the American press. This didn't last long: by 1925 he was back in Asia.

His first stop was China, where he converted to theosophy, and his second Sri Lanka, where he converted to Buddhism. After a spell giving lectures on Buddhism in the US, in 1931 he was ordained in China as a Buddhist monk and given the name Chao Kung. Under this new moniker, he started life as a monk, writing pamphlets and travelling to find new disciples. He was giving lectures in France and Germany in 1932 when he was arrested again, this time for an old debt he owed to the wife of a Dutch consul. Luckily for him, he was found to be insolvent and released, and by the time he got back to Shanghai some months later, he had acquired thirteen followers.

The fact that Trebitsch-Lincoln eventually ended up being a cult leader should not come as a surprise, but his cult falling apart soon enough shouldn't either. While attempting to set up a monastery in Europe with his disciples, Chao Kung and his dwindling band of disciples got rejected from various countries, and by 1937 he was back in China. This really should have been the end of it all, but he still had a few tricks up his sleeve. First, there was the freelancing he did for Japan – at a time when its relationship with China was less than rosy – by writing anti-British propaganda.

Then, when the Second World War broke out, there was the side he took – you can probably guess which. In 1941, SS colonel and attaché to the German embassy in Tokyo Joseph Meisinger visited Shanghai and wound up meeting Trebitsch-Lincoln, who presented him with a plan to help the Nazis in Asia. The idea was for him to become the leader of Tibet and make the Buddhists rise against any British influence left in the area. Somehow, his reputation didn't precede him, and Meisinger took the bait. Shortly afterwards the thirteenth Dalai Lama died, prompting Trebitsch-Lincoln to proclaim himself the new Dalai Lama in a move supported by Japan but – understandably – not by Tibetans.

Meanwhile, the plot was working its way up to high-ranking Nazi circles, with Heinrich Himmler and Rudolf Hess both taking an interest in it. Sadly for him – and as had happened so often in his long, twisted and ultimately disappointing life – it came to nothing in the end, and the Nazis moved on. Or perhaps they didn't. Trebitsch-Lincoln had once sent a letter to Hitler himself denouncing the Holocaust, and it is said that the Nazis then decided to have him poisoned once they managed to invade Shanghai. There is no evidence whatsoever that this is what took place, but in 1943 the former MP for Darlington did die after an operation following some intestinal troubles. In a way, either end would have been fitting; whether finally betrayed by the monsters he associated himself with or gone after a stroke of bad luck, Ignaz Trebitsch-Lincoln arguably got what he deserved.

William Long (?–1426)

MP for Rye, 1410–20

Not a tremendous amount is known about the early years of William Long, which isn't surprising given that they were over six hundred years ago. He was probably born in the 1370s, or perhaps the 1380s if he was especially precocious, and almost certainly grew up around Rye, in the south of England.

What we do know is that he was a merchant in the late fourteenth century, importing wine and exporting wool, but by the early fifteenth century he had decided to turn to a more lucrative line of work: piracy. In 1404 he sailed over to the coast of France and attacked two French ships; in 1405 he plundered a Spanish ship carrying olive oil; in 1406 he helped capture a Prussian ship. Various attempts were made to arrest him but the authorities were getting nowhere, partly because Long was unrepentant and good at what he did, and partly because he often had the support of local coastal communities.

Still, things started getting a bit dicey in 1407 when he captured two Flemish merchant vessels from Bruges, only months after England had signed a truce with Flanders. Some more efforts were made to have him arrested, but to no avail; he spent the rest of the year merrily attacking Breton ships at sea. In fact, he was still doing his thing in October 1410 when he captured two Flemish salt ships. This turned out to be an awkward move as by that point England was in the process of renegotiating its truce with Flanders, which was due to come to an end shortly afterwards. Oh, and Long had become the MP for Rye, which perhaps wasn't the best look.

After some diplomatic brouhaha, Long was still not arrested but it was agreed that the truce would be strictly enforced. Imagine everyone's delight, then, when in March 1411 he captured two Flemish wine ships, as well as a Florentine carrack. Furious, the government ordered the arrest of all pirates who had taken part in the pillaging, as well as anyone willing to harbour or assist them. Amazingly, this did not dampen Long and his crew's spirits, as they went on to capture another fourteen – fourteen! – Flemish ships the following month.

They triumphantly returned to the south coast with tons of plunder, and exchanged their looted wine for meat, bread and everything else they could get, proving that government orders not to deal with the pirates had very much fallen on deaf ears. This predictably infuriated the government, who already had a lot on its plate with the Flemish truce negotiations, culminating in an order to arrest Long and his fellow pirates and confiscate their properties and ships.

After a bit of a game of cat and mouse across land and sea, Long and his ally Sir John Prendergest were finally indicted for treason and felony. Long was thrown into the Tower on 13 June, after which the government finally managed to sign the blasted renewal of the truce with Flanders. But while Prendergest was soon pardoned and merrily off to break the truce with Flanders, Long had to spend nineteen months in prison before getting released by the king, who had heard the famous pirate was feeling repentant. To be fair to him, there is no proof that he ever went back to pillaging and plundering after that, despite receiving a warm welcome home on his beloved south coast, where he remained the local MP.

That did not stop him from returning to the high seas, however, although this time only as a mere merchant, as he had been in his youth. That his ship was attacked in 1420 while carrying wine to Flanders feels like fate; that he was then called before the Exchequer on suspicion of smuggling doesn't feel like too much of a surprise.

As with his early years, we know little of the end of William Long's life. He left Parliament in 1420, and was known to be a tax collector in Sussex in 1421 and 1422. There is no word on what he was up to after 1423, but he did pass away in 1426 in Rye – where else?

George Gordon (1751–93)

MP for Ludgershall, 1774–80

Lord George Gordon was born into a noble Scottish family and educated at Eton. At twelve he joined the Navy, where he eventually reached the rank of lieutenant but failed to rise any further and so turned his attention to other matters in his early twenties. In 1774 he was given the seat of Ludgershall, a pocket borough, and soon became a very annoying member of Parliament.

An outspoken critic of the government, Gordon would also passionately speak out against any faction that had displeased him, and was clearly very fond of the sound of his own voice. His speeches were, according to some usually more diplomatic parliamentary historians, 'extravagant, incoherent, and irrelevant', and his interruptions in the Chamber 'tediously frequent'. In one particular incident in 1780, he decided to read out a long pamphlet in its entirety from the green benches, managing to make around a hundred and fifty MPs leave the Chamber in resigned protest. Undeterred, he attempted to read out the whole thing again the very next day, explaining that it was 'really so excellent that it ought to be read every day in the week'.

Then, in the same month, he accomplished the feat of virtually emptying the Chamber by deciding to read out the Declaratory Act of 1718 in its entirety, for a second time. His fellow MPs were not the only target of his rants; that same year Gordon had also managed to get an audience with the king, in which he spent so much time reading out a pamphlet that the monarch, defeated, had to pledge on his honour that he would finish reading the bloody thing himself in his own time.

This was all tedious enough for everyone involved (apart from Gordon himself), but things were about to take a turn. In 1779 he had founded and started to head the Protestant Association, in order to try and repeal the Papists Act of 1778. On 2 June 1780 he led a crowd of sixty thousand people to Parliament to deliver a petition against partial Catholic emancipation. As you may have guessed, the march turned into what would later be known as the Gordon Riots, which lasted for several days, saw several prisons and banks attacked, a number of Roman Catholic chapels destroyed, and over four hundred rioters killed or wounded by the army.

Gordon was arrested and tried for high treason in 1781 over his role in the riots, but acquitted thanks to a team of talented lawyers. He had, by that point, lost his seat, and considered standing again, then didn't. Instead, he managed to be annoying elsewhere. In 1785 he became convinced that the Pope had sent two Jesuits to England to poison him, and wrote to the Foreign Secretary to demand protection. A year later he refused to bear witness in an ecclesiastical suit, and so was excommunicated by the Archbishop of Canterbury.

This was followed by a bit of a plot twist, as in 1787 Gordon converted to Judaism. He changed his name to Yisrael bar Avraham Gordon, underwent ritual circumcision in a synagogue in Birmingham, and started a happy new life there within the local Jewish community. Sadly, this new chapter was not due to last; in January 1788 he was sentenced to five years in prison for, among other things, a libellous attack on Marie Antoinette and the French ambassador that had been published in the *Public Advertiser*.

He was sent to serve his sentence in Newgate Prison, where he ended up leading a fairly pleasant life. He fasted when the halakha required it, observed Jewish holidays and was given kosher meat and wine by the prison authorities, and was allowed to put a mezuzah on the door of his cell and have the Ten Commandments hung on his wall for Shabbat. A distinguished inmate, he was allowed guests and was always kind to the other prisoners, making him a very popular figure in the building.

In fact, there was widespread concern when he fell ill with typhoid fever in 1793, and after he passed away Charles Dickens wrote: 'The prisoners bemoaned his loss, and missed him; for though his means were not large his charity was great, and in bestowing alms among them he considered the necessities of all alike, and knew no distinction of sect or creed.'

Still, his life ended on a bittersweet note, as fears that his grave would get desecrated in a Jewish cemetery meant that he was buried in the grounds of an Anglican church in Piccadilly instead.

William Parry (15??–85)

MP for Queenborough, 1584–5

William Parry was born in Wales and had twenty-nine siblings and half-siblings, which isn't necessarily relevant but felt worth noting. After attending a local grammar school, he fled to London to try and make a life there, and soon married a reasonably wealthy woman.

After spending some time in the household of the first Earl of Pembroke, he joined the court of Elizabeth I in 1570. Though he had by then married a second, wealthier wife, Parry started having some financial troubles. This probably explains why he sought to go spy on Catholics in Europe soon afterwards, as his creditors would not follow him to the Continent.

Parry came back to England in 1577, only to find that the people he still owed money to had disappointingly not forgotten about him. He left again two years later, secretly joined the Roman Catholic Church, returned in 1580, and was once again faced with increasingly angry creditors.

Since running away hadn't worked, he went for a somewhat more hands-on approach, and assaulted one of them instead. This resulted in a death sentence, which was a low point. Still, he managed to get a pardon from the queen and some sureties for his debts, so things were finally looking up.

This is why it is especially puzzling that in 1582 he went back to the Continent and decided to become a double agent – or did he? After touring Europe and chatting to whoever would listen about his plot to kill Queen Elizabeth, he returned to England and told that very same monarch what he had been doing, explaining that he had been trying to uncover some Protestant plots.

Amazingly, the queen swallowed it and gave Parry the parliamentary seat of Queenborough as a reward. This was yet another point in his life when he could have chosen to go straight, but of course that would have been too easy. Somehow in debt again, Parry concocted a new plot to kill the queen, which he then planned to expose in order to get another reward.

He approached Sir Edmund Neville, a courtier, and told him of his plan to shoot Elizabeth during a private audience, or while she was riding in her carriage. Some sources claim that he did actually intend to murder the monarch by that point, but frankly it's anyone's guess.

What we do know is that Neville told on Parry and that Parry was arrested for high treason, and that this time the queen didn't come to his rescue (and honestly, who could blame her). Parry was expelled from Parliament on 11 February 1585; on 18 February his trial began; and on 2 March he was on a scaffold. In true Parry fashion, he had originally pleaded guilty, then claimed he was innocent, but it was too late.

6

The Assorted Mavericks

A remarkable, an extravagant, a strange, but not what is commonly called a bad man.

Journalist William Jerdan
on Richard Martin

Victor Cazalet (1896–1943)

MP for Chippenham, 1924–43

Despite his obscenely French name, Victor Cazalet was born at 4 Whitehall Gardens, a previous residence of Sir Robert Peel, into the English aristocracy. His childhood home was the Fairlawne Estate in Kent and his godmother was Queen Victoria, who the family would receive as a guest at their villa in France. It will not come as a shock, then, that he was educated at Eton, followed by Oxford University.

When the First World War broke out, he got commissioned into the Queen's Own West Kent Yeomanry, where he eventually became captain, and in 1917 he was awarded the Military Cross for gallantry. After the war ended he spent two years in Siberia, then got himself elected as the Conservative MP for Chippenham in 1924. His own politics were somewhat muddled; he became a prominent supporter of General Franco and actively lobbied for the fascists, but then was one of a small group of MPs who fought against Chamberlain's appeasement policies.

From that point onwards, Cazalet's life can be divided into three main areas of interest. The first one was the creation of a homeland for Jewish people. He started speaking frequently on the topic in 1941, arguing, among other things, that 'on the treatment of Jews, and of all small minorities, depends the future of mankind' and that 'in God's good time the Jewish State will be established and it will contribute as much happiness and prosperity to the Arab as to the Jew'. In 1943 he visited Cairo and Jerusalem, attending a meeting in the latter with the future Israeli PM David Ben-Gurion, where he said: 'I would gladly give my life for the establishment of a Jewish state in Palestine, as I am ready to give my life for the preservation of the British Empire . . . Whatever happens, the Jews must have a permanent home'.

The second was his love of sport, and talent for it. On top of his parliamentary career, he managed to win the British Open Squash Championship in 1925, 1927, 1929 and 1930, and was a member of the English national squash team in 1927. He was also a competitive tennis player, and appeared at Wimbledon seven times between 1922 and 1933.

The third is delightfully random, and started in 1936 when he met Francis and Sara Taylor, an American couple who had recently moved to England and owned an art gallery. Cazalet and the couple became friends straight away, and the Taylors and their daughter Elizabeth started spending their weekends in a cottage on the MP's estate in Kent. Cazalet was very fond of four-year-old Liz, gifting her a horse and taking such good care of her he became her godfather.

When he was warned by Winston Churchill in 1939 that the war was about to start, he told the Taylors to move back the United States as quickly as possible, which they did. Once safely settled in Los Angeles, they kept in touch with Cazalet, who lent yet another helping hand to his goddaughter by introducing the family to Hedda Hopper, an acquaintance of his who was a Hollywood actress and gossip columnist. Thanks to her, the Taylors' new gallery soon attracted a glamorous society crowd, which helped when little Liz decided to get into acting in 1941. And so the decades-long career of global superstar Elizabeth Taylor started.

Sadly, Victor Cazalet did not live to see his protégée take over the world. In 1943 he was involved in a plane crash in Gibraltar that killed all sixteen people on board, including fellow MP John Whiteley.

His death was mourned in many countries; as the *New York Herald Tribune* put it,

> There can be few other Englishmen of our time who have touched so many nations and so many individual citizens upon terms of understanding and friendship . . . It was as an understanding observer and appreciative visitor that Americans held him in affection and will remember him. To that post-war world, which must lean heavily upon men of goodwill if peace and justice are to prevail, Victor Cazalet is a heavy loss.

Victor Grayson (1881–1920?)

MP for Colne Valley, 1907–10

Victor Grayson's life started and ended with a mystery. We know he was born in 1881 in Liverpool, but were his parents aristocrats who had found themselves with an unwanted child? Was he the lovechild of a relative of Winston Churchill and a common woman? No one was quite able to find out.

In any case, he was raised by William and Elizabeth Grayson, one, both or neither of whom he was related to, and had a reasonably modest upbringing. At fourteen, he ran away and managed to get himself onto a ship headed for Australia, but was found out four days into the trip and brought back to England. Instead, he became an apprentice engineer in nearby Bootle in 1899, and discovered the trade union movement.

Despite an early interest in socialism, his life turned towards religion for a few years at the insistence of his mother, and in 1904 he started training to be a Unitarian minister. It was there, in his capacity as a Sunday school teacher, that he discovered his talent for public speaking. Soon enough he applied it to his one true passion: politics. As one of his fellow students at Owen's College in Manchester (an early version of the University of Manchester) put it: 'If the word went round that Grayson was talking in the Common Room we would flock down in crowds . . . it was all socialism, it was a kind of religion with him'.

By 1906 he had left Owen's College altogether and become a prominent public speaker in the Manchester area. A year later, and while still in his mid-twenties, he decided to stand as an independent candidate for the seat of Colne Valley. The move was bold. Though selected by the Independent Labour Party, Grayson failed to gain the endorsement of the Labour Party, as it had an electoral pact with the Liberals in that constituency, and did not want to throw it away on such a young and inexperienced campaigner. Unwilling to back down, he stood as an independent socialist candidate and, to everyone's surprise, won.

The campaign was an interesting one; his electoral platform was revolutionary socialism – one step further than even the Independent Labour Party – as well as votes for women. Though few figures on the left came up to the seat to support him, Emmeline Pankhurst did. It made sense – Grayson didn't mince his words, telling his supporters:

> The placing of women in the same category, constitutionally, as infants, idiots and Peers, does not impress me as either manly or just. While thousands of women are compelled to slave in factories, etc., in order to earn a living; and others are ruined in body and soul by unjust economic laws created and sustained by men, I deem it the meanest tyranny to withhold from women the right to share in making the laws they have to obey.

Once in Parliament, Grayson did not keep quiet. In a matter of months he managed to alienate pretty much everyone else on the left and got himself suspended from the Commons for rowdiness in the Chamber. In fact, he all but lost interest in what was taking place in Parliament pretty fast, preferring to travel up and down the country making speeches about socialism instead. He also had a drinking problem that became more and more of an issue, and the sort of cushy lifestyle that looked out of place for a socialist firebrand.

As a result, the people of Colne Valley voted him out in 1910. He tried and failed to win the seat of Kennington after that, and kept struggling with his health. After a brief but ultimately unsuccessful attempt to get sober in 1913, he found himself, a year later, married, a father, and still an alcoholic. He also lost all support from fellow left-wing politicians that year for supporting the start of the First World War and encouraging young men to join the army, which very much was a minority view among socialists.

In 1917 he somehow found himself joining the New Zealand Army, as he had been making speeches there, and fought at Passchendaele where a shrapnel wound in his hip got him discharged again. His life went from bad to worse a year later when wife Ruth gave birth to another child, who died minutes after being born, then passed away herself four days later.

Things were looking bleak for Victor Grayson, and were about to get even bleaker. In that same year Basil Thomson, the head of Special Branch, convinced himself that the former MP was someone they needed to keep an eye on. He instructed one of his agents, Arthur Maundy Gregory, to start spying on Grayson, as 'he always spells trouble. He can't keep out of it . . . he will either link up with the Sinn Feiners or the Reds'. This is where things get confusing again.

What we know for certain is that Gregory did spy on Grayson, and that Grayson was, at that point, living a rather grand life in central London despite not having the income to back it up, and after some years of living in relative poverty. Was Gregory giving money to Grayson? Was Grayson involved in some criminal activities? It remains unclear to this day.

In any case, Grayson found out in 1919 that he was being observed and set out to dig up some dirt on his own personal spy, and by 1920 he had found out that Gregory was selling honours on behalf of Prime Minister David Lloyd George. Though keeping it to himself may have been a safer move, the socialist decided to go public instead, declaring publicly: 'This sale of honours is a national scandal. It can be traced right down to 10 Downing Street, and to a monocled dandy with offices in Whitehall. I know this man, and one day I will name him.'

In what should be a thoroughly unsurprising (though worrying) turn of events, Grayson was beaten up on the Strand just a few days later – by whom, we can only guess. Refusing to be intimidated into silence, he kept giving speeches on the honours scandal (which, in fairness to him, actually was taking place, and would later turn out to be a rather big deal).

It all came to an abrupt end on the evening of 28 September, when he was out with friends in central London. After receiving a phone call, he told his drinking companions he had to go to the Queen's Hotel in Leicester Square but would return shortly. He never did. In fact, he was never seen again. Was he killed by the state for his knowledge of the honours scandal? Did he disappear, then live the rest of his life elsewhere, under a false name? Did something even shadier happen between Grayson and George? No one knows. Victor Grayson's life ended the way it started – with countless questions and no answers.

Praise-God Barebone (1598–1679)

MP in the Barebone's Parliament, 1653

The frustrating thing about Unless-Jesus-Christ-Had-Died-For-Thee-Thou-Hast-Been-Damned Barebone is that it is unclear whether Unless-Jesus-Christ-Had-Died-For-Thee-Thou-Hast-Been-Damned was his name, his brother's name, or even his son's name, although everyone does seem reasonably certain that there was, at one point, a Unless-Jesus-Christ-Had-Died-For-Thee-Thou-Hast-Been-Damned Barebone with a relative named Jesus-Christ-Came-into-The-World-To-Save Barebone.

Sadly for us, Praise-God Barebone did not lead a life whimsical enough to really deserve a full entry in his book, but his name – was it his name? – did need to be noted. It should also be pointed out that he was involved in the Nominated Assembly in 1653, which became known as the Barebone's Parliament. That they did not decide to fully embrace him and call it Unless-Jesus-Christ-Had-Died-For-Thee-Thou-Hast-Been-Damned Barebone's Parliament is, frankly, a disappointment.

Christopher Monck (1653–88)

MP for Devon, 1667–70

Christopher Monck was the son of the first Duke of Albemarle and he did not waste any time. After a private education, he entered Gray's Inn at the age of nine, then became the MP for Devon at the age of thirteen. He joined a number of committees in the Commons and was a reasonably active MP at first. In fact, he made his first speech in the Chamber at fifteen, which is thought to still be a record.

His father died in 1670 and he inherited his spot in the

House of Lords but was too young to take it, as peers had to be at least twenty-one. Still, he did become a Knight of the Garter and a Privy Councillor, as well as the lord lieutenant of Devon and a (titular) colonel in the English Army.

He also had some amusing hobbies, including boxing or, as it was still called at the time, 'pugilism'. In fact, he arranged a boxing match between his butcher and his butler in 1681, which was the first ever fight to be recorded.*

In 1686, Monck was appointed governor of Jamaica and he left for the island the following year. Though he did not really achieve anything worthy of note there, he did get involved in the recovery of the wrecked Spanish treasure ship *Nuestra Señora de la Concepción* the year he arrived. The expedition was the first successful salvage operation in modern times, and made Monck an even wealthier man.

Sadly, he did not have much time to enjoy the funds, as he died a year later from a combination of alcoholism and struggles with the warm weather. He was thirty-five.

Richard Martin (1754–1834)

MP for County Galway, 1801–12

MP for County Galway, 1818–26

Born into a wealthy Irish family in County Galway, Richard Martin was educated in England, first at Harrow School and

---

* If you were wondering, the *Protestant Mercury* tells us that the butcher won the prize, as though he was 'but a little man', he was 'the best at that exercise in England'.

then at Trinity College, Cambridge. After leaving university he embarked on a grand tour, which took him and his friend throughout Europe, then to Jamaica and finally to New England, where the pair witnessed the beginning of the American War of Independence. Upon his return he was admitted to Lincoln's Inn in 1776 and entered the Irish House of Commons the same year, where he sat for seven years, then again from 1798 to 1800.

He was, by that point, a famous and talented duellist known as Hairtrigger Dick, after the nimbleness of his fingers on the pistol. There are many stories about his exploits, but it is hard to know how much truth there is to them. It was said, for example, that at the start of a duel he would open his shirt to reveal a large wound on his chest from a previous encounter, look his opponent in the eye and say 'Your target, sir!'

Tragically, his duelling career came to an end when he got himself embroiled in a family dispute with his cousin and close friend, James Jordon of Resolven. Though Martin wanted to resolve the issue peacefully, Jordon insisted on a fight; Hairtrigger aimed low, in an attempt not to cause too much damage to his opponent, but to no avail. He shot him in the upper leg, and a week later Jordon died from the infected wound. Heartbroken, Martin had been heard wailing 'No! I could not have missed him. Poor Jordon, I could not have missed you!' after the event, and decided to put an end to his duelling ways.

Luckily, he had other things to be getting on with. In 1801 he arrived in Westminster as the new MP for County Galway. Quick-witted and not scared to draw attention to himself, he soon became a known figure in the Commons. According to a contemporary account:

Martin is not a very learned man, neither is he, in the language of the schools, eloquent, but he has a most winning way with him. He holds the House by the very test of the human race, laughter, and while their sides shake, their opposition is shaken and falls down at the same instant. There is a beautiful symmetry, a perfect keeping, as it were, in the whole man . . . every limb of his body and every feature of his face is round and solid. He lets drive at the House like a bullet and the flag of truce is instantly flung out upon all sides.

Martin's passion was animal rights, but let's put that aside for a moment – first, we must discuss the events that took place in the summer of 1821. King George III was due to visit Dublin in August, and so a group of assorted Irish dignitaries went to Liverpool and hopped on the *Earl of Moira*, a steam packet ship. The voyage got off to a very poor start as the weather was bad and the departure had to be delayed. It went rapidly downhill after that as the captain, who had been drinking before setting off, kept drinking on board, and was no longer able to stand up one hour into the journey.

As the storm worsened, the captain refused to turn around, and instead the ship hit a sandbank and got so damaged there was no option but to wait for the high tide to return. In the end, dozens of people and two horses died in the shipwreck, and fewer than twenty passengers survived. Thankfully, Martin was one of them – which brings us back to Parliament.

Martin's passion was animal rights – he had been trying to change the law to protect creatures from human harm for some time. All his early efforts had failed, but 1822 saw the passing of the Ill Treatment of Cattle Bill, also known as Martin's Act. 'An Act to prevent the cruel and improper Treatment of Cattle', to give it its full name, was one of the first pieces of legislation relating to animal welfare passed anywhere in the world. Not content with having changed the law, however, Martin wanted to make sure people knew about it too, and was ready to put in the work himself.

In a case that soon became famous, he went down to Smithfield market and had two men arrested there for mistreating their horses. His new-found hobby of prowling the streets of London trying and find people harming animals and bringing them to court for it soon made him a target for mockery in the press, but that did not stop him.

What nearly did put an end to his campaigning was a trip on the *Alert* in the spring of 1823, when the vessel was reported lost at sea. The news prompted the Duke of Bedford to note that he was 'glad to see old Dick Martin of Galway is dead: he has long been a general nuisance, public and private', but ol' Hairtrigger had managed to survive yet another shipwreck. Back in Parliament, he kept trying to fight against animal cruelty, but did not manage to get anything as revolutionary as Martin's Act through the House of Commons.

Sadly, he had also found another passion by this point: gambling. When he was unseated in 1826 following accusations of illegal intimidation during the election campaign, Martin realised he was now at risk of being in legal trouble for his gambling debts, and he fled to France. He spent the last of his years in Boulogne-sur-Mer, and, despite having been mocked for it at the time, was soon remembered as a man who had effected great change. As journalist Samuel Carter Hall later wrote:

> He blundered his way into a reform, blessed in its influences and mighty in its results . . . Thus the wild, energetic, heedless and usually unreasoning Irishman is for this Act classed, and rightly so, among the benefactors of his country and all the countries of the Old World and the New.

John Townsend (1819–92)

MP for Greenwich, 1857–9

John Townsend was born in Deptford and was the son of a successful estate agent and auctioneer. His first passion was acting, which he started doing at twelve with the company of Edmund Kean, a famous Shakespearean stage actor. In 1841 he married actress Sarah Mitchell and in 1842 he leased the Theatre Royal in Richmond, where he specialised in Shakespeare plays.

Sadly, acting and putting on plays did not turn out to be especially lucrative. By 1852 he had given up on it altogether to take over the family business, and had found an interest in politics instead. In that same year he was the agent of the Liberal candidate in Greenwich, who won the seat, and a few years later he founded the local Liberal Association.

His fondness for campaigning required more money than he could afford, and in 1857 he was both elected as the new MP for Greenwich and found to be bankrupt. Despite being given more time to pay off his debts by his creditors, he was declared bankrupt again in March 1858. This was a serious issue, as he had cast several votes before informing the House of his financial situation; they were found to be illegitimate and were disallowed.

While unable to sit in the Chamber or vote, Townsend was given twelve months to get his house in order. His attempt to pay back his creditors brought him back to the stage, and he appeared in various playhouses across London as 'John Townsend, MP'. Despite being reasonably popular and, among other things, playing Richard III on horseback (thought to be the last actor to do so) at the Greenwich Literary Institution, he soon announced that he would be standing down from the Commons altogether.

He took the Chiltern Hundreds in February 1859, putting an end to his burgeoning political career. Perhaps it was for the best; after a short stint as the manager of the Theatre Royal in Leicester, John, his wife and their seven stage-trained children moved to Canada. Though the original plan was to buy land and take up farming, the Townsends soon went back to their favourite trade.

At first, Sarah and the couple's eldest daughter started performing together in an amateur company in Upper Canada. Soon enough, John returned to the stage as well, and after that the whole family started performing together in a local playhouse dubbed 'the Theatre Royal'. The Townsends were popular actors, and after stints in Ottawa and Hamilton, they spent a decade touring southern Ontario and the northern United States as 'The World Renowned Townsend Family Star Dramatic Troupe'.

John's health started to decline and he left the travelling

company in 1877 to become an elocution and acting teacher in Hamilton. One of his students was Julia Arthur, who went on to become a globally famous stage and film actress. He died of liver cancer in 1892, in his adopted home of Western Ontario. There, he was remembered as a leading character in the industry, who helped launch many local theatre companies and was one of the first Canada-based company managers to pioneer tours in the United States.

Mabel Philipson (1886–1951)

MP for Berwick-upon-Tweed, 1923–9

As you may have noticed, there have been few women in this book. There are a number of reasons for this, most of which were outlined in the introduction, but it is cheering to know that some female MPs did manage to be out of the ordinary, even in the first few decades in which they started appearing in Parliament.

One of them was Mabel Russell. Born in Peckham, south London, to a dressmaker and a travelling salesman, the early years of her career had nothing to do with politics. Her first job out of school was at a theatre box office in Clapham, from which she graduated to be an understudy, then a fully fledged theatre actress. Skilled on stage, she soon became famous in the capital, and appeared in starring roles in a number of plays.

In 1911 she married Thomas Stanley Rhodes, but sadly the couple were involved in a car accident only six months later, which killed him and blinded her in one eye. This did not put an end to her career, and it was only at the height of her fame in 1916 that she decided to give up on acting. Mabel had always wanted a family, and finally found one when she married Scots Guard lieutenant Hilton Philipson a year later.

A plot twist came in 1922 when the army man decided to try and get into politics. Philipson stood as a National Liberal candidate in Berwick-upon-Tweed with the support of David Lloyd George, but unusually fighting against another candidate from the Liberal Party. Though he did win by a comfortable margin in November, an election petition was lodged against him the following January, alleging that he had overspent during the campaign. The accusation was found to be shaky, but despite being found innocent, Philipson was not allowed to stand in the seat again for seven years.

Instead, the couple came up with a plan: Mabel could stand in the by-election herself, then hand the seat back to her husband once he was legally able to take it again. Her one condition, however, was that she would be standing as a Conservative, which showed that she wasn't simply intending to be a placeholder. Quick-witted, good with the public and genuinely interested in the constituency, Philipson proved to be an impressive campaigner, and managed to gain the seat that had been Liberal for nearly forty years.

She was also the third woman ever to win an election and take up her seat in the House of Commons, after Nancy Astor and Margaret Wintringham. The by-election had been closely followed nationally, and it was noted that Philipson was a somewhat more colourful character than her two predecessors, as this limerick shows:

> *Lady Astor, MP for sobriety,*
> *Mrs Wintringham; She's for propriety,*
> *Now Berwick-on-Tweed*
> *With all speed has decreed,*
> *Mrs Philipson wins – for Variety.*

Though she was never fond of making lengthy speeches in the Chamber, Philipson became a dedicated constituency MP, with a particular interest in agriculture, the needs of ex-servicemen, housing and women's issues. Most of her work took place in committees, including the Joint Select Committee on the Guardianship of Infants Bill 1923 and the Air Committee in 1925. In 1924 she joined a parliamentary delegation to Italy, where she met Pope Pius XI and Benito Mussolini. The only woman on the trip, she caught the eye of the latter, who nicknamed her *la bella* Russell, after her maiden name.

In 1927 she drew the ballot to present a private member's bill, and chose a topic she had been campaigning on already. Thanks to her Nursing Homes Registration Act 1927, nursing homes had to be registered and were subject to frequent inspections. And, because she was a woman of many layers, she used parliamentary recess that year to return to the stage to play in a run of *The Beloved Vagabond*.

Still, politics was never a long-term career choice for her, and when her husband decided in 1928 that he was no longer interested in standing for Berwick-upon-Tweed, she announced her resignation, saying that 'the reason why I have held the seat has ceased to exist'. After the election of 1929 she returned to acting for a time, with some success. She had a prominent role in the then-famous comedy *Tilly of Bloomsbury* in 1931, amusing the director by calling him 'Mr Speaker' in rehearsals.

After a few more roles, she left public life for good in 1933, finally deciding to do what she had been wanting to do for so long; be a mother and take care of her family. She died in a nursing home by the seaside nearly twenty years later, having lived quite a life after all.

A true maverick, Philipson paved the way for eccentric women becoming members of Parliament. Here's to hoping that in a few decades' time a book like this one will be published on the weird and wonderful women who followed in her footsteps.

Acknowledgements

I would like to thank my couch, on which I wrote the entirety of this book. I would not like to thank the COVID-19 pandemic, which forced me to spend several months alone on my couch writing this book.

I also must thank my agent Imogen Pelham and my editor Joe Zigmond and the whole team at John Murray, as without them I would have spent the COVID-19 pandemic on my couch with nothing to do.

Chapter opener pictures, Alamy Stock Photos: Chapter 1/ Chronicle, Chapter 2/Colin Waters, Chapters 3, 4 and 5/ Granger Historical Picture Archive, Chapter 6/World History Archive.

Bibliography

Antrobus, D., *A Guiltless Feast: The Salford Bible Christian Church and the Rise of the Modern Vegetarian Movement*, City of Salford Education and Leisure, 1997

Burke, J., *A General and Heraldic Dictionary of the Peerage and Baronetage of the British Empire*, 4th edition, 2 vols, Henry Colburn, 1833

Caesar, E., 'House of Secrets: Who Owns London's Most Expensive Mansion?', *New Yorker*, 23 May 2015

Cash, A. H., *John Wilkes: The Scandalous Father of Civil Liberty*, Yale University Press, 2006

Chisholm, H., 'Heber, Richard', *Encyclopædia Britannica*, Cambridge University Press, 1911

——, 'Huskisson, William', *Encyclopædia Britannica*, Cambridge University Press, 1911

——, 'Portland, William Henry Cavendish Bentinck, 3rd Duke of', *Encyclopædia Britannica*, Cambridge University Press, 1911

Clark, D., *Victor Grayson: Labour's Lost Leader*, Quartet Books, 1985

Clarke, E., 'Slaney, Robert Aglionby (1792–1862)', *Oxford Dictionary of National Biography*, Oxford University Press, doi:10.1093/ref:odnb/95468

Cook, M., Mills, R., Trumback, R. and Cocks, H., *A Gay*

History of Britain: Love and Sex between Men since the Middle Ages, Greenwood World, 2007

Cowing, E., 'The Red Duchess and the Dirtiest By-Election in History', *Scottish Daily Mail*, 21 February 2017

Dakers, C., *A Genius for Money: Business, Art and the Morrisons*, Wiley, 2012

Dale, I., Smith, J. and Trevelyan, A., *The Honourable Ladies*, vol. 1, *Profiles of Women MPs 1918–1996*, Biteback, 2018

Debrett, J., *An Asylum for Fugitive Pieces . . .* Printed for J. Debrett, 1785

Donaldson, W., *Brewer's Rogues, Villains and Eccentrics: An A–Z of Roguish Britons through the Ages*, Phoenix, 2004

Downes, M., *Pugilistica: The History of British Boxing Containing Lives of the Most Celebrated Pugilists*, J. Grant, 1906

Ferris, J. and Thrush, A., *The History of Parliament: The House of Commons 1604–1629*, Cambridge University Press, 2010

Fisher, D. R., *The History of Parliament: The House of Commons 1820–1832*, Oxford University Press, 2009

Garfield, S., *The Last Journey of William Huskisson: How a Day of Triumph became a Day of Despair at the Turn of a Wheel*, Faber & Faber, 2003

Gillen, M., *Assassination of the Prime Minister: The Shocking Death of Spencer Perceval*, St Martin's Press, 1973

Goffin, M., *The Watkin Path: An Approach to Belief*, Sussex Academic Press, 2005

Graham, R., *Mogreb-el-Acksa: A Journey in Morocco*, Good Press, 1898

——, Papers of Robert Bontine Cunninghame Graham, 1852–1936, University of Glasgow Special Collections, GB 247 MS Gen 512/27–29

Gribbin, J. and Gribbin, M., *FitzRoy: The Remarkable Story of Darwin's Captain and the Invention of the Weather Forecast*, Yale University Press, 2004

Groves, R., *The Strange Case of Victor Grayson*, Pluto Press, 1975

Haddelsey, S., *Operation Tabarin: Britain's Secret Wartime Expedition to Antarctica, 1944–46*, History Press, 2014

Hasler, P. W., *The History of Parliament: The House of Commons, 1558–1603*. Boydell & Brewer, 1981

Hayton, D., Cruickshanks, E. and Handley, S., *The History of Parliament: The House of Commons 1690–1715*, Boydell & Brewer, 2002

Hayward, J., *Myths & Legends of the First World War*, History Press, 2011

Headingly, A. S., *The Biography of Charles Bradlaugh*, Freethought Publishing Company, 1888

Henning, B. D., *The History of Parliament: The House of Commons 1660–1690*, Boydell & Brewer, 1983

Hitchens, C., Reader, He Married Her, review of *Tom Driberg: His Life and Indiscretions* by Francis Wheen, *London Review of Books*, vol. 12, no. 9, 10 May 1990

Hodgkins, D., *The Second Railway King: The Life and Times of Sir Edward Watkin 1819–1901*, Merton Priory Press, 2002

Kavanagh, K., *Born without Limbs: A Biography of Achievement*, Family Publications, 1989

Kettle, M., *Salome's Last Veil: The Libel Case of the Century*, HarperCollins, 1977

Knox, J., *Legge, Edward, Dictionary of National Biography*, Smith, Elder & Co., 1892

Knox, W., *The Lives of Scottish Women: Women and Scottish Society 1880–1980*, Edinburgh University Press, 2006

Lees-Milne, J., *Harold Nicolson: A Biography*, 2 vols, Chatto & Windus, 1980

Leyland, S., *The Men Who Stare at Hens: Great Irish Eccentrics, from W. B. Yeats to Brendan Behan*, History Press, 2019

McCormick, D., *The Incredible Mr. Kavanagh*, Devin-Adair, 1961

McGrath, P., *John Whitson and the Merchant Community of Bristol*, Bristol Branch of the Historical Association, 1970

McKenna, N., *Fanny & Stella: The Young Men Who Shocked Victorian England*, Faber & Faber, 2013

Michell, J., *Eccentric Lives and Peculiar Notions*, Argonaut Books, 1984

Namier, L. and Brooke, J., *The History of Parliament: The House of Commons 1754–1790*, 3 vols, Boydell & Brewer, 1964

Niblett, B., *Dare to Stand Alone: The Story of Charles Bradlaugh*, Kramedart Press, 2011

Nimrod (Charles James Apperley), *Memoirs of the Life of the Late John Mytton, Esq*, Rudolph Ackermann, 1837

Norton, R., 'Homosexuality in Nineteenth-Century England: A Sourcebook', rictornorton.co.uk, 2015

O'Shea, J., *Prince of Swindlers: John Sadleir MP*, Geography Publications, 1999

——, 'Sadleir, John (1813–1856)', *Oxford Dictionary of National Biography*, Oxford University Press, doi:10.1093/ref:odnb/95468

Phillips, P., *Humanity Dick: The Eccentric Member for Galway*, Parapress, 2003

Rhodes James, R., *Bob Boothby: A Portrait*, Hodder & Stoughton, 1991

——, *Victor Cazalet: A Portrait*, Hamish Hamilton, 1976

Roberts, S., *Sir Benjamin Stone 1838–1914: Photographer, Traveller and Politician*, CreateSpace, 2014

Rose, N., *Harold Nicolson*, Jonathan Cape, 2005

Roskell, J. S., Clark, L. and Rawcliffe, C., *The History of Parliament: The House of Commons 1386–1421*, Boydell & Brewer, 1993

Rothschild, M., *Dear Lord Rothschild: Birds, Butterflies and History*, Hutchinson, 1983,

Scrivener, P., *Mad Toffs: The British Upper Classes at their Best – and Worst*, Metro, 2016

Sedgwick, R., *The History of Parliament: The House of Commons 1715–1754*, Boydell & Brewer, 1970

'Sir A. Crosfield's Fall from Train', *Manchester Guardian*, 30 September 1938

Sitwell, O., *Left Hand Right Hand*, Peter Smith Publishing, 1975

——, *Tales My Father Taught Me*, Michael Joseph, 1962

Smith, D., *The Peer and the Gangster: A Very British Cover-up*, History Press, 2020

Spear, J., *Of Jews and Ships and Mob Attacks, of Catholics and Kings: The Curious Career of Lord George Gordon*, Pennsylvania State University Press, 2002

'Swerved to Avoid Child, Killed', *Northampton Mercury*, 1945

Taylor, A., *The People's Laird: A Life of Robert Bontine Cunninghame Graham*, Tobias Press, 2005

Thomas, P., 'John Wilkes', *Oxford Dictionary of National Biography*, Oxford University Press, doi:10.1093/ref:odnb/95468

Thorne, R., *The History of Parliament: The House of Commons 1790–1820*, Sidgwick & Jackson, 1986

Topham, E., *The Life of the Late John Elwes, Esquire: Member in Three Successive Parliaments for Berkshire*, John Jarvis, 1790

Tucker, S. D., *Great British Eccentrics*, Amberley Publishing, 2015

Walker, C., *Oliver Baldwin: A Life of Dissent*, Arcadia Books, 2003

Ward, J. W., *Letters to 'Ivy' from the First Earl of Dudley*, Longmans, Green, 1905

Ward-Jackson, P., 'Lord Ronald Gower, Gustave Doré and the Genesis of the Shakespeare Memorial at Stratford-upon-Avon', *Journal of the Warburg and Courtauld Institutes*, vol. 50, 1987

Wasserstein, B, *The Secret Lives of Trebitsch Lincoln*, Yale University Press, 1988

Wheen, F., *The Soul of Indiscretion: Tom Driberg, Poet, Philanderer, Legislator and Outlaw*, Fourth Estate, 2001

Wilson, H., *The Book of Wonderful Characters: Memoirs and Anecdotes of Remarkable and Eccentric Persons in All Ages and Countries'*, J. C. Hotten, 1869

Wright, E., *History's Greatest Scandals: Shocking Stories of Powerful People*, Allen & Unwin, 2006